BASKETBALL
MY WAY

BASKETBALL MY WAY

by
NANCY LIEBERMAN

WITH
MYRNA & HARVEY FROMMER

Photos by Kimberly Butler

Charles Scribner's Sons   **New York**

Copyright © 1982 Nancy Lieberman

Library of Congress Cataloging in Publication Data

Lieberman, Nancy, 1958–
  Basketball my way.

  Includes index.
  1. Basketball for women.   2. Lieberman, Nancy,
1958–   . 3. Basketball players—United States—
Biography.   I. Frommer, Myrna.   II. Frommer,
Harvey.   III. Title.
GV886.L45   796.32'38   81-21223
ISBN 0-684-17012-4   AACR2

1 3 5 7 9 11 13 15 17 19 F/C 20 18 16 14 12 10 8 6 4 2

Printed in the United States of America.

For Lou and Eva Saks,
my grandparents,
who never wanted me to practice at P.S. 104
and from whom I now get my strength.

—Nancy Lieberman

For Jennifer, our athletic daughter,
who also played at P.S. 104.

—Myrna and Harvey Frommer

Contents

Contents

Contents

Contents

BASKETBALL
MY WAY

Part One

THE LIEBERMAN PHILOSOPHY

Basketball Is My Life　1

I was born on the first day of July in 1958. Contrary to some stories you may have heard, I wasn't born with a basketball in my hand, and I didn't take my first few steps while dribbling a ball. I was born in Brooklyn, New York, but, when I was just a baby, I moved with my father and mother and brother Cliff to Bayswater, a neighborhood in Far Rockaway, in the borough of Queens.

The house we lived in was designed by my father, Jerome Lieberman, but he did not spend much time in it. He left my mother, Renee, soon after we moved in. Being without him was rough on all of us. My mother had the sole responsibility of raising my brother and myself. Cliff was asthmatic, studious, a lover of music, while I put all my energy into sports. Maybe it was for attention—my father's attention. I don't know. For a long time I was terribly bitter. I guess just going out and playing ball was the way I was able to forget it, because after a while I never worried about things like that.

My first real game was football. My mother would look in the yard and see a pile of helmets and bodies, but no Nancy. I was

3

under the pile, and my mother stopped my football playing very quickly.

Then I turned to basketball. I was not allowed to play in the Public School Athletic League because I was a girl, so I found other areas where I was allowed to play. I competed against the boys at the YM–YWHA in Far Rockaway. I also went down to the beach and, with the ocean as a backdrop, played more basketball against boys. I used to look for any game in any place. I played "radar ball" at night in the neighborhood playgrounds. There were distant streetlights that gave off a glow, but you could hardly see the basket. But that was fine with me. It helped me develop my shooting touch. Night after night I would practice or play games of one-on-one with friends.

By the time I was fourteen, when my parents were divorced, I must have already spent a million hours on basketball. I thought about it, I played it, and I dreamed a dream of making history in it. I was an oddity for many—a girl playing in what had always been a male-dominated sport. I guess a little Jewish girl who dressed in cutoffs and had a comb stuffed in her back pocket and a wad of gum in her cheek was not your typical basketball player. But I didn't care what people thought of me. I just wanted to play basketball.

I was a New York Knickerbockers fan, and my idols were Willis Reed, Walt Frazier, and Dave DeBusschere, numbers 19, 10, and 22, respectively. I admired Reed's power and desire, Frazier's cool, penetrating style of play, and De Busschere's leadership and steadiness.

When women did play basketball while I was growing up, they played mainly in a nonaggressive style. For years the image most people had of women basketball players was one of girls in skirted tunic outfits shooting underhand from between their legs. However, I did things on the court that other women had never done before, so there were many who claimed that I played like a man. I dove for the ball. I penetrated. I banged my way up for the boards. I tried to intimidate, to steal, to use all I had to prevail on the court.

During all of this I had many battles with my mother. "Please

Nancy," she would scream, "give it up. Come in for dinner. There's no future in basketball for a girl. Why don't you want to be a nurse or a secretary? You'll never get anywhere on a basketball court." She was so infuriated with my love for basketball that one day she took a screwdriver and punctured my basketball. But even that didn't stop me from playing.

I played on the Far Rockaway High School basketball team, and in my sophomore year we lost the city championship by only one point. When I was a junior I would travel by subway all the way up to Harlem to play on the AAU team, the New York Chuckles, coached by LaVozier LaMar. They called me "Fire." The high school guys I played against used to yell "face job, face job" at each other after I did something against them on the court. I had no trouble on the streets of Harlem—nobody ever bothered me. I guess my scrappiness on the basketball court had become well known.

In my junior year I also played for Far Rockaway High School and for the St. Francis De Salle's CYO team. My De Salle team won the CYO title. Far Rockaway High School was disqualified because of my CYO playing, since each team could not have its participants playing for another team and be eligible for competition. In my senior year, my Far Rockaway High School team reached the quarterfinal of the city championship.

Some of the best times of my life were spent playing playground ball. The guys were always bigger and rougher than me. So I tried hard to be mean and hard-nosed. I had to learn to get around the pole in the schoolyard. I had to be able to take their elbows and give them back measure for measure. We'd play five-on-five, and it was a thrill to be chosen over guys. When they complained, I gave them the lip right back, which led to a lot of fistfights. I had to earn their respect by showing them that I was capable of playing as well as they did. I learned every aspect of the game in high school, in the playgrounds, on the AAU team in Harlem. I studied the game and worked to make myself as proficient at it as possible. When the basketball season came to an end, it seemed as if my life came to an end too.

During the off-seasons I would practice indoors in the house.

It drove my mother crazy because I would get fingerprints on the ceiling while working on my jumping ability. I told her, "Mom, one day I'm going to make history."

Some people say I already have made history. I hold fifteen school records and have won two straight Wade trophies as the outstanding women's college basketball player. I am happy that I was the most widely recruited high school women's basketball player and that I helped Old Dominion College win two national championships in 1979 and 1980. At the start at Old Dominion, attendance at our games was perhaps 350. Gradually, more and more people came out. When we played the Soviet Union, there were 10,000 people there.

The honors and awards have been gratifying, and they'll stay with me a long time: youngest member of the 1976 Olympic basketball team, which won the silver medal in Montreal; MVP First Annual All-American Basketball Classic; holding my own against men in the 1980 New York Summer Professional League, the premier summer league, and playing in the same backcourt with Nate "Tiny" Archibald. I did not play in the summer league as a stunt. Another woman might have been embarrassed, but I was not out there to showcase my guts. I was there to make myself a better player. It was a great thrill to be the number one draft choice of the Dallas Diamonds in the Women's Professional Basketball League.

I think back to those nights of "radar ball" and my mother's complaints and my admiration for Walter Frazier, whose number 10 I wore when I starred at Old Dominion and still wear now with the Dallas Diamonds. And I'm glad that I've been able to buy my mother a Cadillac. All these things are part of the record, but they are also in the past. Now I look to the future. There's a lot more history that I want to make.

1. Playing in the New York Summer Professional League (1980)

Caring for Yourself 2

Over the years I have had my share of disappointments, bruises, periods of fatigue, downs as well as ups. I have taught myself how to handle these things, how to keep myself in the best possible shape so I can play the best possible ball. There is no magic formula. I do not believe in the wonders of astrology, the cop-out of drugs, the artificial boosts of liquor, the mind control of hypnosis, or any of the other fads and pitfalls that some people get themselves into. I believe in clean living. I believe that if you take care of your body and your mind, they will take care of you. For an athlete to mess around with drugs or liquor or to abuse herself in any way is suicidal, to my way of thinking. I'd like to share some thoughts with you on conditioning, nutrition, and mental attitude. They've worked for me; I know they'll work for you.

CONDITIONING

An athlete who is not in shape is an athlete who is bound to get into trouble. If you lack the proper muscle tone, the durability, the extra energy that basketball demands, you will not only find that you are ineffective on the playing court, but also prone to injury. A tired player is one who is unaware of her limits and is vulnerable to injury. Even though basketball is called a non-contact sport, there's plenty of contact in the game today. If you get knocked to the ground and you're in condition, you can take the pounding. If you get knocked to the ground and you're not in shape, there is a good chance of being seriously injured. And the hurt takes a much longer time to heal. That's another one of the reasons that I am so very much in favor not only of working on conditioning but working on continuous conditioning. It distinguishes the top athlete, the basketball player who can perform at top speed most of the time, from others who are just going through the motions.

During the playing season, you'll be exercising enough and getting enough playing time to be in shape. Your coach and/or trainer will probably suggest all types of things concerning your weight and endurance. One thing, however, that is often overlooked is pregame warmups. Your body is like an automobile. It takes a lot out of a car if you begin driving it at high speed the minute you get into it. Therefore, it is important that you prime your body for high-speed performance on the basketball court. To do this, pregame calisthenics are essential. Work on exercises that stretch your body. Get all your joints as loose and flexible as you can. Work on your arms, legs, neck, hands, and fingers. Limber up. Stretch your arms out to your sides, then bend down, alternately touching your left toes with your right hand and your right toes with your left hand. Do this about ten times. Spread your feet as wide as possible and twist them in and out, adding and reducing pressure to tone muscles. Bend from your waist. Such techniques get your torso, legs, back, and waist loose and ready. During game conditions you may find that certain parts of your body are not as loose as other parts. This may be a tip-off that you did not devote enough time in the pregame calisthenics to the conditioning of those areas. Learn from this experience and make a mental note to exercise that part of the body a bit more next time.

The proper amount of sleep and rest is a very crucial part of conditioning. Everybody likes to have fun and do all kinds of exciting things. Part of the dues one pays for succeeding as an athlete is to know when to withdraw from such activities in order to get the proper amount of rest or sleep.

I believe in eight hours of sleep a night. You can determine your own hour to go to sleep and rise, but try to set a pattern of the same time each day and night. It gets your body regulated on a biological clock. Although eight hours of sleep work well for me, this is not a hard and fast rule. All of our bodies work with different rhythms. You may find that you need nine hours or ten hours, seven or six hours—you be the judge. The important things that you should be aware of are the demands athletics make on your body and to give your body a chance to recuperate from those demands.

NUTRITION

There's a saying that claims "You are what you eat." Experience has taught me that this is true. As an athlete, I burn up a tremendous amount of energy, which requires a diet rich in vitamins and minerals. Consequently, I eat a lot, and I try to see to it that the food I consume is of good quality. I work on eating three balanced meals a day, and avoid eating between meals as much as possible. I drink a great deal of liquids—water and fruit juices, and I don't recommend soft drinks as part of a regular diet. There isn't much food value in a lot of water and sugar. My general diet is high in protein: broiled meats, fowl, fish, whole grains. A lot of fresh fruits and vegetables are also a part of my daily menu. I try to avoid rich and fatty foods and limit my consumption of sweets. I'm not a health-food fanatic and every once in a while I do enjoy eating foods that are just delicious, whether they're especially nutritious or not. However, I do maintain a healthy, nutritious diet most of the time. I am 5 feet 10 inches tall, weigh 146 pounds, and maintain this weight consistently.

I also supplement my diet with vitamins. I am a big fan of vitamin C in chewable form, which helps prevent colds and other respiratory problems. There are many other vitamins on the market, and each one has a special function. Your doctor or trainer should be consulted to decide which ones are appropriate for your needs.

Don't look for a magic formula where nutrition is concerned. Three squares a day—of good quality—lots of liquids, vitamins to give you an extra boost—this about sums up the Nancy Lieberman philosophy of nutrition.

ATTITUDE

The difference between a winner and a loser is many times a matter of inches. The difference between a winner and a loser is many times a matter of mind. If you think you can do it, most of the time you'll do it. I have a very positive feeling about playing basketball. I try to do my best and think I'll do my best every time I'm out there competing on the basketball court. If my team loses or if I have a poor performance, I consciously try not to take the game home with me. I don't brood and I don't make excuses. I don't blame the opposition by saying they were too good. Nor do I blame my own teammates by saying they were not good enough. I just make a mental note that there will be another game, another chance, another day coming up, and I'll be able to balance things out then.

Brooders, sulkers, and egotists have the mark of the loser about them. Winners have a realistic, positive attitude about them. If you get down on yourself, you'll have trouble getting up again. Keep at an even keel. Remember, every game has a winner and a loser, but every game starts at a score of 0–0 for each time and each player.

If you triumph, don't showboat, crow, brag, or rub it in on the other team and its players. Athletes don't forget. Doing this is like waving a red flag at an enraged bull. The only thing you will accomplish is getting the opposition psyched up so that the next time you meet, they'll be going all out to get you. I definitely do not mean that you should not play the game hard, as hard as you can. But once you have won, ease up and be a graceful winner.

Common sense is a wonderful and often ignored attribute. If you abuse yourself and your opponents, you pay a price. If you take care of your body with the right foods, vitamins, conditioning, sleep, rest, and pregame calisthenics, you will benefit and reap the rewards. If you are a gracious but tenacious performer, you will gain the respect of your teammates as well as your opponents.

Injuries 3

I have found that the most common types of injuries that take place early in the season are shin splints and blisters. You can generally prevent blisters by wearing two pairs of wool socks and by applying some type of skin toughener to your feet. I don't recommend cotton socks; they don't have the same type of power to cushion as do woolen socks. Many players pick up shin splints—an inflamed muscle between the shin and the foot caused by a good deal of running on a hard surface. One way to reduce the problem of shin splints is to do a lot of running during the off-season, especially on grassy surfaces. Avoid running on a floor with a hard surface since this is not much better than running on a gym floor. It is much easier to prevent shin splints by taking precautions and conditioning than it is to treat the condition once you have it.

You'll find that a lot of wear and tear will take place on your ankles, knees, and fingers. It is very important that you follow the advice of your trainer about treatment. Don't be a hero. Don't play in pain if you don't have to since you may be risking a permanent injury. If there is no trainer around when you sustain an injury, be guided by a few practical tips to take care of your own needs. I have found that the use of ice and elevation of an ankle or knee work wonders. Elevation decreases arterial flow; pressure on the injury with ice also decreases arterial flow as well as venous flow. Ice will keep the swelling to a minimum, but always apply it covered with some type of protection—an ice bag, a thin towel, etc. Raw ice will give you frostbite.

Equipment 4

If you are engaged in some type of organized basketball activity, all the equipment you need will be provided—the ball, the uniform, possibly even sneakers and socks. If you have these things, the main thing to keep in mind is how to make the most of them.

Before I take the court for a game, I always make sure that my sneakers are laced up so that my feet feel comfortable in them. It is an annoyance and a distraction to have your laces come loose during a game. By pausing to tie them, you break your concentration and that of your teammates. It is also a very uncomfortable feeling when you sense or anticipate a lace coming loose.

Socks should also fit comfortably. Different players have different thoughts on how high up socks should rest on the shin. You will have to decide what is best for you. The higher (within reason) the socks, the more protection you provide against floor burns. Whatever the height of your socks, they should be fitted to your feet so that they do not slide down and bunch up as you play your game. Try putting some baby powder on your feet before you go on the court. A little powder makes my socks feel more comfortable.

Check your uniform in all types of movement positions: jumping, stretching, passing, running, bending. If your shorts come up on you or you feel a sleeve pulling under the arm, get a larger size. If you think a uniform projects your image and you are more concerned about the way it looks than the way it feels, you are making a mistake. Comfort is much more important than looks when playing in a game that needs your total concentration.

A sweatband is an additional piece of equipment that may be useful for you. You probably have noticed some players who wear headbands, which, I think, is more for image than for practical value. However, sweatbands or wristbands are very valuable. You can wear one or two—whatever feels comfortable for you. Sometimes, when you are heavily perspired and stepping up to the foul line with wet hands, the only dry spot on your body is your wristband. Use it to dry your hands so you can shoot your foul shot with more confidence and comfort.

When playing ball, jewelry of any kind is something you can do without. In practice and game situations remove earrings, rings, watches, chains, bracelets, etc. You may have seen professional players on television wearing some elegant adornments. I don't really approve of this. You can hurt yourself or another player with jewelry. If you are moving at top speed, jewelry can function like a weapon. So play it safe and save your jewelry for when you get dressed up.

Part Two

OFFENSIVE SKILLS

Shooting 5

Shooting and scoring is a part of the game that is probably enjoyed more by younger kids when they're learning how to play than any other phase of the game. You very seldom see kids working on defense. They grow up wanting to shoot the ball and to score points. And scoring points is the name of the game. So let's consider that glamorous part of basketball—shooting the ball.

Confidence is of prime importance. You have to believe in yourself, that when you shoot the ball it's going to go in the basket. This kind of confidence is particularly essential when one shot can determine whether or not you win the game. In this case you would want the basketball to go to someone who has confidence in her scoring ability.

Concentration is also extremely important. In shooting the ball, you must be able to block out everything else from your mind. You must pretend there is no one else on the court, and you must forget that there is a defensive player. Block it all out—except for your technique, your aim, your concentration.

Balance is a big aid to shooting the ball correctly. For example, when you shoot a jump shot, you should be able to jump straight up and land in the same general area that you left the floor. Then you know your body is in balance and that you're not leaning one way or the other, either backward or forward.

Different parts of the body play different roles in shooting. The head should be turned toward the basket, and the shoulders, hips, and feet should also be squared straight with the basket. If you turn your shoulders one way in shooting the basketball, the ball will likely go off in the direction in which you're turned. If your hips are opened to your right, for example, chances are your shot will be pulled to your right. Squaring straight to the basket brings your body in a straight line with the basket. Concentrate on the target while taking aim. Don't watch the arc of the basketball. Watch the basket.

Be certain to keep your elbow in when shooting the basketball. To find out whether your elbow is in, let your arms hang straight down by your body. Then swing your shooting arm straight up, hand back, and place the basketball into your hand with your arm cocked. Now you know that your elbow is in. This is important because, by keeping your elbow in, you'll be shooting the basketball straight. If your elbow is back or to your side, you'll be pushing the basketball more than shooting it. And chances are the ball will go off if your hand is crooked and not in a straight line.

Rest the basketball on your fingertips, not the palms of your hands. This will give you a good feel for the ball and ensure that you are getting good backspin. When you release the basketball, be certain to follow through. Do this as though you're putting your hand right inside the basket and picking something out of it.

ASPECTS OF GOOD SHOOTING

There are three important parts in the process of shooting. Naturally, the first one is body alignment. Make sure your body is lined up straight with the basket. The second important part is that your shooting hand be straight in line to the target. Remember, this means that your elbow is in. The third involves

2. Gripping the basketball for a shot

the way in which you are gripping the basketball, holding it for the shot. Let's imagine you are a right-handed shooter. The fingers of your right hand should be spread behind the basketball, and your left hand should be placed gently to the side of the ball so that you are using it strictly for guiding purposes. See Illustration 2. When you are ready to release the basketball, bring it back and cock it. When you start to follow through, releasing the basketball for the shot, take the guiding hand off the basketball. The shot is completed with your right hand. Follow through, arm straight, hand as though it were dipping over your head into the basket.

POINT OF AIM

There are three different approaches you can take regarding the point of aim. Some people say you should aim for the back of the rim. If you're short and aim for the back of the rim, the ball will be a straight-in shot. If you're long and aim for the back of the rim, you'll have a chance to back in the shot.

A second approach states that when you catch the basketball and square up, you really don't have time to zero in on any particular part of the rim. You zero in on the complete basket. Probably the most logical and natural place to zero in on is the front of the rim since you are trying to get the basketball up in the air and just over the front of the rim. I think this is the best place to focus on when you bring the ball up to shoot the shot.

The third approach focuses the point of aim on the backboard. This is a very important factor in the art of shooting. Naturally, depending on where you are on the floor, it is sometimes much easier to shoot the basketball with the aid of the backboard. If you are straight on, it is much more difficult to try to bank the basketball off the backboard because the basketball comes off at such a bad angle. If you are to the side of the basket, using the backboard will take some of the force off the shot so that it kisses the glass and then travels to the rim. It is now a much softer shot. You have a better chance of the ball staying on the rim and possibly dropping in. A straight shot, on the other hand, is going to hit the rim and bounce off. The backspin that you put on the ball will help decrease the angle of the rebound when it comes off the basket. That's because the backboard really cuts down on the backspin that the basketball has. Backspin helps compensate for the effects of a ball hitting too hard against the backboard. If there's a lot of backspin on the ball as it hits the glass, it cuts down on some of the force. So, using the backboard can really help keep the basketball alive on the rim, and you have a better chance of the ball falling for you.

Another important area that ties in with the point of aim and use of the backboard is the arc of the basketball when you release it in flight. Do not shoot the basketball in a straight line. Instead, get the basketball up in the air so that it will travel on a downward path, giving it a much better chance of going into the basket. Naturally though, the higher the ball is in the air, the more difficult it is to control.

TYPES OF SHOTS

The Lay-up

The first of the several different types of shots in basketball we'll talk about is the lay-up. This is the shot that should be taught to kids first. The lay-up is one of two easy shots in the game of basketball today. The easiest shot is the foul shot from the free-throw line because no one is guarding the shooter. The lay-up is simple because the shooter is so close to the basket. In practicing shooting lay-ups, remember that you are high jumping to the basket and not broad jumping. The idea is to jump up, not out, to the basket to make the shot a shorter shot. In fast breaks, many times a person goes in for a lay-up and jumps too soon. She jumps out too far from the basket, shoots the basketball, and comes down out of the play. If the shot is missed, she's out of the play and out of a position for a rebound. So it's important to jump high up to the basket, making it a short shot. Then come down right by the basket, because you're able to rebound if you missed the shot.

Many kids approach the lay-up from a very poor angle, or they

3. The lay-up shot

release the ball from their chests or their shoulders and not up above their heads. They also might have poor extension of the arms, an improper release of the guide hand, or they place the shooting hand over the ball so that when the ball hits the backboard it is still traveling in its upward flight.

It is essential when approaching the basket for lay-ups that you don't look down at the ball. This requirement is similar to the principles of proper dribbling: keep your head up so that you are able to see exactly where you need to take off from the floor; know where you are the whole time. You see kids watching the basketball, watching the dribble, looking down at the floor. When they finally decide to pick the ball up to shoot the lay-up, they find themselves under the basket and caught in a bad angle from which to shoot. It is very important to keep your head up and see exactly where you're going.

Another important thing to keep in mind is that a lay-up is a short jump shot. It is not shot underhand. A lot of times you will see kids shooting the ball underhand almost as though they're lobbing the ball to the basket. This is not good practice because if the defensive player hits the shooter's hand, she does not have a chance to get the ball up to the basket. Shooting a jump shot or a one-handed set shot and using your nonshooting hand as a guide protects the basketball from the defensive player. If she takes a swing at the basketball, the defensive player will hit your guide hand, which is between her and the basketball. Then you're still able to get the ball up to the basket.

When you approach the basket for a lay-up from the right side, you should be shooting the basket with your right hand. Face the basket going in at an angle in which you are able to put the ball up on the glass in the square. By doing this you are allowing some of the force of the shot to be taken off so that the ball will lay on the rim and fall in easily and softly. When you approach the basket, you're coming in, and you must push off on your right foot to jump off your left foot. Plant your right foot, push off to your left and then go up off your left. I must emphasize this is a high jump and not a broad jump; you want to jump up to the basket to shoot the basketball.

If you are on the left side of the basket, again be sure your steps are correctly understood. Coming in, you are planting your left foot, pushing off it, shifting your weight on to your right foot, and now jumping off your right foot up to the basket—a high and not a broad jump.

The Power Lay-up

Another type of shot is the power lay-up, which is executed from a dribble or a received pass. You land with both feet on the floor and jump up toward the basket as hard as you can so that if, by chance, a player bumps you or knocks you off balance, you still are able to shoot the shot on balance. An extra plus in this shot is that you come down in good rebounding position if you miss the shot.

Always use the backboard on lay-ups. Never go in for a lay-up from the front of the rim because it is such a difficult shot. Always try to get to the left or the right side of the basket so that you can use the backboard at a better angle and be positioned for a rebound.

The Set Shot and the Jump Shot

The set shot is considered the long shot of basketball. The jump shot is used for close in where you're jumping up and shooting the basketball in traffic. But a set shot is shot when the defense is back away from you and you have time to shoot, and when you're at a greater distance from the basket. The set shot is released like a jump shot. Square up your head, shoulders, hips, and feet to the basket, knees bent, and on the balls of your feet. Follow through with your elbow in and your arms straight as though you were placing your hand inside the basket. This is much easier to learn than the jump shot because you have much better body balance.

The jump shot has changed the game of basketball today. Years ago when the game was invented and through the early 1960s, the jump shot did not have much of a place in the game. You made a lay-up or shot a hook shot or a set shot. But we have such good athletes today that the jump shot can be shot from various areas on the floor—from short range, where you're jumping up over your defensive player, medium range, or even long range.

4. The jump shot

Today many athletes work hard on all types of jump shots because they're so closely guarded at all times, and they don't practice their set shots. Because this shot is released at the peak of the jump, all the force must be exerted from the shooting hand. Thus, greater strength is necessary for this shot. It's not really that important how high you jump. Some coaches believe it's important to jump as high as you can to release the ball at your peak; others feel that the shot is just a shot, that it should be released at your peak regardless of how high you jump. From my experience I've learned that the important thing is to shoot the basketball at your peak regardless of how high you're jumping. In shooting the jump shot, be conscious of shooting and coming down in the same place. This ensures proper body balance.

The Hook Shot

Used most exclusively by pivot players, the hook shot is very similar to the hook pass. You will see it usually in the lanes around the basket because it is such a difficult shot. You must keep your body between the ball and the defensive player so that she cannot block the shot. The hook shot may be executed from a stationary position or following a dribble. For a right-hand hook shot, the player steps to her right with the left foot crossing the body. At the same time she rotates and tilts slightly back to the left. Look over the left shoulder for point of aim for this shot. The ball is held in the right hand in a horizontal plane. The right arm is extended and brought up overhead. When you release the basketball, again follow through as though you have your hand right inside the basket.

Because this is such a difficult shot it should not be taught to youngsters. It is almost impossible to defend against because the shooter always has her body between the basketball and the defensive player. The shooter needs several feet of space to get off the shot. It cannot be shot in traffic.

We're starting to see a new shot being put into traffic—the jump hook. The player uses the same type of body technique but jumps straight up and hooks the ball over her head. This shot keeps the body between the defensive player and the basketball

5. The hook shot

and allows the shooter to come down in a desirable position so she can rebound if necessary.

The Tip-in Shot

The tip-in shot occurs when a teammate shoots the ball and it comes off the basket just slightly off the rim, and you are able to jump up and control the basketball. Cradle it on your fingertips, and tap it right back into the basket. The player must have good rebounding position in front of the basket. Control of the basketball is crucial to execute this shot. Knees, hips, and ankles must all be flexed. Your hands must be right up, ready to catch the ball. Do so in such a way that you can keep your body as much as possible between the defensive player and the ball when the rebound comes off. If you don't block the defensive player away from the ball when it comes off, she can easily hit your arm.

The Free Throw

To me, the free throw is the easiest shot in basketball—bar none. Nobody is guarding you, and the shot really comes down to confidence and concentration. You should have confidence in your ability to shoot a free throw no matter what the situation. Block out everything else. Concentrate on the basket and make the shot. In making the foul shot it is important to find a spot on the foul line where you feel comfortable. Usually it means if you're right-handed you put your right toe smack in the middle of the foul line, splitting the basket right in half. That way you're sure that when you bring your right hand up you're positioning the basketball with your elbow in a direct line with the basket, splitting the rim right down the middle. Be relaxed. Bend your knees. Square up with your feet, your knees, hips, shoulder, and head—square up right to the basket. It's important that you create a rhythm at the foul line. If you're used to going to the foul line and bouncing the ball three times before you shoot it, you need to form a pattern and rhythm in which you do this every time you shoot the basketball.

Free throws are shots that are not given enough emphasis. I think many coaches and players take this shot for granted

6. Getting up for a tip-in shot

because there are no defensive players involved. They'd rather work on techniques and situations where there is constant defensive pressure on the offensive players. But too many games are won and lost on the foul line. It is important you practice foul shooting every day.

One good procedure to use after you receive the ball from the official is to check to see that all your teammates are in their proper positions. Take a couple of dribbles so you develop a pattern or rhythm. Take a deep breath to relax and concentrate on getting the ball over the front of the rim. Develop a good follow-through. Put your hand right in the basket as you follow through.

DRILLS

There are several drills for lay-up shooting. Put five or six players in two lines, one on one side of the basket, the other on the other side and back at the 5-second mark. Have the players on the shooting line with the basketball. The first player will dribble in to the basket and, working on fundamentals, shoot a lay-up. The first woman on the other side will get a rebound and dribble to the back of the shooting line. The shooter will then go to the back of the rebound line so that everyone will be switching lines and taking turns at shooting lay-ups.

Another drill is to have players at the same line with just one basketball in the hands of the rebounder. The shooter cuts to the basket and receives a pass from the rebounder. When the shooter receives the ball, she does not put the ball on the floor to dribble it. Instead, she must go straight up for the lay-up. The passer will rebound and switch lanes. The give-and-go is another drill. Using two lines, the player with the ball passes to a player on the other line and cuts to the basket. The player in the other line takes the ball and passes it back to the shooter who takes a lay-up. Then the two players switch lines.

A good drill to work on when you're alone is to practice making as many lay-ups as you can in 30 seconds or a minute. Shoot a lay-up on the right side. Catch it out of the net. Go over and shoot on the left side. Catch it out of the net. Then shoot with the right hand. Continue this back and forth, being conscious of good body balance, technique, fundamentals, and using the backboard to take force off the basketball.

To practice shooting the set shot, get a teammate to rebound. As you move to different points on the floor, catch the basketball while practicing good fundamentals and body balance. After shooting move to a different spot on the floor. The rebounder catches the basketball under the net or gets the rebound. She then makes a good pass to you. When you catch the basketball, you're square to the basket and you shoot it again. This drill may also be worked on with the jump shot.

Another good drill is to have a contest in which you must shoot ten shots from different points on the floor. Then your teammates take the same ten shots from the same points on the floor. Compete to see who makes the most shots.

Yet another good shooting drill is a game called "21." Here you can get two to five players at each basket with one basketball. Each player in turn takes a long shot from behind a designated spot and follows her shot up with a lay-up. A long shot that is made counts two points. A lay-up counts one point. If both shots are made, the player has another turn. The first player to reach 21 points wins.

Playing "horse" is still another drill. Place two to five players on a basket using one ball. The first player shoots any type of shot from any place on the court. If the shot is made, the next player must attempt to make the same shot. If she fails, she is given the letter H. Every time a player misses following another player's successful shot, she receives another letter until the word HORSE is spelled out. Once the word is spelled, that player is eliminated from the game. The game is over when only one player remains.

An excellent shooting drill is called forty squat jumpers, a squat jump being a jump shot or set shot without a dribble. Place two players together at a basket with a basketball. The passer and rebounder is the same person. You take the rebound from a shot and make a good pass to the shooter, who catches the basketball and squares up and shoots a set shot or jump shot without dribbling the basketball. Shoot eight times and then rotate so the shooter becomes the rebounder–passer, and the rebounder–passer becomes the shooter. Do this in five different sets until each player has shot forty different shots. Once this is done in squat jumpers, you can do it with set shots, or practice dribble jumpers or dribble set shots. Here once the shooter receives the basketball, she may put it on the floor once or twice and move to another spot, and then square up to the basket and shoot. All of the drills that can be used for the set shot can also be used for the jump shot.

Hook-shot drills are basically the same drills used for the lay-up. You can also practice dribbling across the lane and shooting the hook shot from one side of the lane to the other. Do this just as you would when making a post move in the lane, coming across from one side of the lane to the basket. Another drill especially appropriate for the hook shot is pivot-player practice. You work with the pivot player posting up and down in the low post. A passer is on the wing. She passes the basketball inside to the post player who now shoots the hook shot without a defensive player. Once this is mastered, add a defensive player.

There are several good tip-in drills. One is the 3-in-1 drill where the rebounder stands underneath and in front of the basket roughly 3 to 5 feet away and tosses the basketball up against the backboard. She jumps up when it comes off, cradling the basketball on her fingertips, and taps it back off the backboard three times. As she goes up on the fourth time, she cradles the basketball and taps it back into the basket. In sum, what you have is three taps off the board and a tip-in on the fourth. This can be done 3–1, 4–1, 5–1, or even 6–1. Once this shot has been worked on with the right hand, move to the left side of the basket and work on it with your left hand.

Another good tip-in drill is known as the "Annie Over" drill. It can be practiced with two, three, or four players. Start the drill with two players, one on each side of the basket. The player with the basketball jumps up and shoots the ball over the basket off the backboard to the other side of the basket. The teammate on the other side jumps up and catches the basketball, cradling it on her fingertips, and taps it back over the basket off the backboard to the teammate on the other side. This drill is continued back and forth for 30 seconds to a minute. Once it is mastered with two players, add a third. Put two players on one side of the basket, one on the other. The first player holds the basketball on the side with two women, puts the basketball up off the backboard to the other side of the basket. After she does so, she returns to the floor and moves to the inside, to the line on the other side and gets in back of that line. The teammate on the other side has caught the basketball. She taps it back over to the third player and then moves to the inside and lines up behind the player she was tapping to. This is a continued process. The drill can also be done with four players, two on each side. It keeps you in constant movement, and all players must work on controlling the basketball and tapping it.

Free-throw drills can be done by pairing up. One player shoots two free throws and the other player rebounds. Rotate competitively and shoot anywhere from 25 to 100 free throws apiece. It is a good idea to record all the free throws made each day in practice to evaluate your progress. It is also always good to practice shooting in one-on-one situations. The shooter must be conscious of making the basket in order to be awarded the second free throw.

In still another drill, you can call one player out from a team. If she misses the free throw, everyone on the team has to run. If she makes it, no one has to run. What this does is create peer pressure.

Following conditioning is an excellent time to work on free throws because the body is tired and it takes more concentration to make the shot. Each player should make anywhere from one to three throws before she leaves practice. If she cannot make it, coaches should make her stay until she does.

Footwork 6

Without question, footwork is one of the most important parts of the game of basketball because it is basic to body control and balance. Without it very few other fundamentals can be effectively learned. Footwork refers to the ability to start and stop quickly, change directions, pivot, and perform other techniques essential to the game. Speed is also very important; exceptional speed can be a great asset in making quick starts.

Many players automatically start a move in a correct manner but don't know how to carry it out. Whenever you start it is important that you have your head down and your shoulders lowered so that you're able to push off your back foot and start your move. You must take short, quick steps until complete forward momentum is gained. Move at a pace where you can stop quickly and efficiently without loss of balance. Beginning players with poor body balance may be forced to move at a considerably slower pace than they are capable of. They must do so in order to avoid losing balance and to prevent fouls and violations.

STOPS

Basically there are two ways in which a player can come to a stop: the two-step stop and the jump stop. With the two-step stop one foot lands first, followed by the other in a forward–backward stride. Your feet are 2 to 3 feet apart. This stop is suitable when the defense is not harassing the offense and when the player is in scoring territory. With a quick pivot after receiving the ball, the player may drive or shoot immediately. Most coaches recommend that players on the right side of the court use the right foot as a pivot and those on the left side of the court use the left foot.

In the jump stop, the entire surface of both soles of the feet make contact with the court at the same time. Spread your feet 2 to 3 feet apart. This ensures good body balance, and you can use either foot as the pivot foot.

Often in basketball, an offensive player is forced to change directions to avoid defensive pressure. Change of direction from a running movement has to be very quick. When a player wishes to cut to the right, for example, she plants her right foot and pushes sharply off it, lowers the right shoulder, and then pushes out off the left foot on to the right foot. She continues to move quickly.

PIVOTS AND TURNS

There seems to be little agreement on the differences between pivots and turns. For our purposes, the terms can be used interchangeably. During any turn the ball must be protected and kept close to the body. In a simple pivot, all you are doing is keeping one foot in contact with the floor at all times. Making sure you do not slide, you are able to turn around in a circle maintaining one foot in the same position on the floor. Pivoting is an important maneuver because it enables you to keep the basketball away from the defensive player. By keeping your body between the ball and the defensive player, she will be unable to smack it away from you.

7a. Pivoting. When pivoting to the right, keep your right foot in contact with the floor.

7b. Turn your body, stepping with your left foot across your right foot.

When passing, face in the direction of the pass. This can be accomplished by using the simple turn. Come up and catch the basketball. If you're going to pivot to your right, keep your right foot in contact with the floor. Turn your body, stepping with your left foot across your right foot, and pass the basketball. The right foot remains in contact with the floor at all times. For the reverse pivot, plant one foot in between your opponent's feet. Turn your head and lower your opposite shoulder as the pivot is made. The opponent should be kept outside your hip so that as the free leg is swung around, you can move past her. The free leg swings about 180 degrees, and the player continues to move in the desired direction. The pivot can also be used to post up or to free a player to receive a pass against an overplaying defender. Always keep your body between the defensive player and the ball. That is the most important aspect of pivoting.

DRILLS

Drills can be used to improve footwork. For starts and stops, spread your players out across the end line. Have them run as fast as they can. When they hear the whistle, they must practice the two-step stop. Or let them run at half speed, and at the sound of the whistle practice the jump stop. They can dribble around the court and come to a two-step stop or a jump stop. At this point they can practice pivoting—the reverse or straight pivot.

Another drill is to have two columns of several players on each side of each basket. One column is in the guard position and the other is in the low-post position. A player in the guard position passes to a pivot player moving from low- to high-post position. The pivot player uses a jump stop. She now passes to the next player in the guard position. This can be continued over and over. Players can exchange positions if they desire. Also, the column can be moved from the low position to the wing position. The wing runs up to receive a pass in a stride position and continues doing this same drill, rotating lines.

The "toe-taps" drill is excellent for improving footwork. Run in place as fast as you can on your toes. Note how many times your feet will touch the floor in a period of 30 seconds to a minute. This will increase coordination and speed.

In another drill, start at the end line in a defensive position and run, practicing defensive slides up and down the court. Stay down low in a defensive position. Slide your feet, pretending you're cutting off your man on one side back and forth all the way down the floor. Try to move your feet as quickly as you can without crossing them. Then practice the same drill crossing your feet, trying to run and cut your man off. Again, work as quickly as you can.

Yet another drill involves standing on the sidelines, facing the line. In a period of 15 to 30 seconds see how many times you can jump back and forth across that line. Do the same drill turning sideways, facing at a different angle; then turn and try it from the other side. Once this has been mastered with one line, attempt it with two lines. Each line should be approximately 15 inches apart. Next, you may want to have a big square and divide it into four smaller squares. Jump from one square to the next square, covering all four squares as quickly as you can. First do this facing the squares; then turn and jump sideways from one and then the other direction. The idea is to jump the lines and move your feet as quickly as possible. This will increase foot speed.

To improve agility in footwork, the following drill is useful. Start in a defensive position. Run in place in toe-tap manner. When the coach or a teammate points in a certain direction, do a quarter turn quickly in a defensive position and turn back again facing straight ahead. Remain in a defensive position, tapping quickly. Concentrate on foot speed.

Receiving
the Basketball 7

I don't think that many players devote enough attention to this part of the game. Yet, it is very important because in order to do something with the basketball, you first have to be able to catch it.

By going out to meet every pass, you will cut down the defensive player's chance of intercepting a pass to score the other way. In receiving, it is important that you step toward the ball and catch it with your hands, using your fingertips. Try not to let the ball hit the palms of your hands.

If you're closely guarded and going to receive a pass, position your body between the pass and the defensive player. To do this, you must learn how to get yourself "open." There are several ways to accomplish this. First, you can run a V-cut (see Chapter 12), fake the opposite way from the passer, take a couple of quick, hard steps to drive the defensive player away from the ball, and then cut back sharply, keeping your body in between the defensive player and the pass you are receiving. Another way of getting yourself open if you're closely guarded is to take a couple of steps into the defensive player. This will make her stand up straight. Then you should break back to the ball. A third way of getting open is to take one step toward the defensive player. She'll generally back up. You can then break back to receive the ball.

DRILLS

There are several drills that can be used to develop your ability to receive the basketball. Of prime importance is the development of "good hands," which is essential for being a good receiver.

One drill that you can do by yourself is to throw the basketball off a wall and catch it, paying close attention to how you use your hands. Start your throwing from a distance and slowly move in closer to the wall until you're 3 or 4 feet away. Use force in throwing the ball. A second drill utilizes two people. Both should stand 12 to 15 feet away from the wall. One player throws the ball off the wall, and the other catches this "pass." Both players will slowly move in toward the wall so that the passes are coming off quicker and harder. The receiver has to adjust to the varying speed of the ball as it comes off the wall. The ball can also be thrown at different angles, so that the receiver will have to catch the ball over her head, reach down below her waist, snare the ball at chest level, and so on. It is important in doing this drill that the receiver be forced to move about a lot and become conscious of catching the ball regardless of the speed with which it is thrown.

Fast Breaks ⑧

No basketball team today can be successful without the transition game, or the fast break game. A team cannot get all its points on a set offense. An effective fast break gets the ball off the defensive board and down to the offensive side of the court before the defending team can get set. Control is very important. The philosophy of the fast break is simply to outnumber the other team on offense. Strive to take a good percentage shot and score points.

There are five important components of the fast break: (1) rebounder; (2) outlet passer; (3) middleman or point guard; (4) trailer; (5) safety. Each player in the fast break has a specific role.

REBOUNDER

Good rebounders who limit the other team to one shot are crucial. They should be able to block out the opponent and go up and get the ball. The rebounder must get rid of the ball to the open part of the floor as quickly as possible. Her job is helped by guards who fan out to the foul line extensions the instant the rebound comes off.

OUTLET PASSER

The quick pass off a defensive rebound to a guard streaking down the floor is one of the great attack weapons in all of basketball. When this play is properly executed, I think it is also one of the nicest ones to watch. The rebounding player should be very careful as she throws the ball to a teammate. The basketball should be thrown high enough and hard enough so that it is not intercepted by the defense and possibly turned into an easy two points for the opposition. The player prepared to receive the outlet pass should indicate her readiness by raising an arm. Precision on the part of the rebounder in passing the ball and on the part of the guard in catching the ball and going for the hoop make the outlet pass an excellent example of team basketball. Over the years the Boston Celtics have made the outlet pass one of their chief offensive weapons.

MIDDLEMAN OR POINT GUARD

The fastest player and best ball handler generally takes this guard position. She has to be in control, taking the ball down the middle of the floor as quickly as possible. She should be able to "see" the entire court. It is the responsibility of this player to feed the ball to a teammate or to take the shot. Wing players must get the ball to the middleman at the top of the key. They must outrun her, moving along the foul line extensions. A quick cut to the basket, usually to the corner of the backboard, enables them to receive the ball from the middleman for a quick jump shot.

TRAILER

The secondary player in the fast break is the trailer. She trails to the left side of the middleman. Control is important. The trailer should be ready if necessary to stop at the foul line and take a jump shot. The trailer should also be able to fill the spot of a wing player who has moved out to the corner; she should also be positioned so that she is able to move in quickly for a rebound.

SAFETY

The last player to come down the floor, the safety guards against the other team stealing the ball and coming down the floor to make an uncontested basket. Once the safety sees that the defensive team has not been able to disrupt the fast break, she should race to any vacant spot on the court and be heads up, looking for a pass and a possible opportunity to take a shot.

Communication is very important in the fast break. Generally two players are left inside—the rebounder and one forward. The other players have streaked on down the court. The two players who are left back should communicate and decide who plays the role of the safety and who plays the role of the trailer. Most often the rebounder is the safety, and the big forward, if she trails the fast break, should move out to the left side of the middleman.

OTHER TYPES OF FAST BREAKS

Some teams use the sidelines fast break, moving the ball quickly up one side of the floor. Once the guard has flared to the outside, she takes the basketball up the side quickly. The guard with the ball should look for the other guard who has filled the opposite side. I don't recommend the sidelines fast break. It diminishes scoring opportunities since it limits your offense to one side of the court.

Some teams use the designated lane or organized fast break. One player is assigned to bring the ball up the middle of the floor. She does this by moving to the foul line or top of the key area once the rebound is made and looks for the outlet pass. The other guard fills the right side of the floor as quickly as possible. The left lane is filled by your quick forward. The fourth player is the trailer. The No. 5 player is the safety. It is important that the No. 1, No. 2, and No. 3 players get to the same spots each time. This simplifies things and makes for more control.

A variation on the organized fast break can be used after a shot is made by the opposition. Your team's forward gets out of bounds and shovels a pass from the right sidelines to the No. 1 player at the top of the key. The No. 4 player functions as a safety on the left side in case the No. 5 player has trouble getting the ball in. From this point, the same responsibilities exist for all players as with a missed shot.

A fast break can be executed after a free throw. This can be done in the same manner as the organized or designated lane fast break, or a variation can be executed. Guards flare to the side for the pass from the rebounder. When one guard gets the pass, the other breaks to the top of the key for a return pass from the first guard. The quick forward fills the opposite lane. Communication among all players is necessary. They should tell each other who has what role.

DRILLS

The best fast-break drill involves a center and a guard. Emphasis should be placed on making the good rebound, the good outlet pass. A good drill involves a rebounder and two guards. The nonreceiving guard must fill the top of the key and obtain the return pass. A third drill utilizes four players: practice should stress the outlet pass and the players filling their lanes. Proper position, scoring techniques, and percentage shots should be worked on. You can add defensive players and work on all types of combinations: two-on-one; three-on-one, four-on-one, four-on-two, and so on. Keep adding and subtracting players, practicing all the possible game situations.

In a two-on-one drill, two offensive players go full court against one defensive player until the offense scores or the defense stops the play. Whoever shoots the ball then plays defense against the other two players. The same routine is used for three-on-one and four-on-one drills.

In a four-on-two drill, four offensive players go full court against two defensive players. The player who shoots the ball and the player who passes the ball then play defense against the other four players.

The five-on-three is a great fast-break drill and conditioning drill. Five players start at half court and go nonstop for a specific period of time (3 minutes, 5 minutes, etc.). Three defensive players are positioned at each end of the court. If the offense scores, they take the ball out of bounds and the ball is thrown in to the outlet. The wings fill the lane and the offensive goes five-on-three at the other end. If the five players miss their shot, they must continue to try for the shot until it is made or they are stopped cold by the defense. The groups then switch.

Passing 9

Getting the ball to the open player and piling up assists is a part of "inside basketball" that wins games. The passing game involves much more than just throwing the ball to a teammate. There are different passes for different game situations. Some are more important than others, but all of them should be learned. You never know which one you might have to use. The following are the main types of passes.

TWO-HANDED CHEST PASS

Even though this pass is not used that much today in game situations, it is the first pass that should be learned because it stresses fundamentals.

The basketball should be on your fingertips. Step in the direction in which you are passing the ball and throw to your receiver so that she will catch the ball in her chest area. Don't throw the pass in such a way that the receiver has to reach over her head or below the waist to catch it. If you make a good pass to the receiver, she should be able to catch the ball and to set in a triple-

8. Two-handed chest pass

threat position—that is, she can either shoot, dribble, or pass the ball.

When you throw the pass, keep your elbows in. When you step, follow through and turn your hands to the outside for proper backspin on the ball. It is important that you step toward the receiver when you pass the ball, just as it is important that the receiver step toward the passer. The pass should also be thrown at a speed that allows the receiver to handle the basketball.

There are some simple drills to aid you in practicing the two-handed chest pass. If you're by yourself, use a wall where you can work on the fundamentals of the pass. Draw a little square on the wall and pretend this is your teammate's chest. Try to throw the pass to the square. When practicing with a teammate stand 10 to 15 feet away. Pass the ball back and forth and work on fundamentals again. In this drill you're also able to work on receiving the ball.

A third drill can position one player in the guard area and another in the wing area. Practice techniques in which the wing player gets open or free and the guard makes effective chest passes. Two players can also practice by starting at the baseline and spreading themselves roughly 10 feet apart. Go down the floor passing the ball and working on catching the two-handed chest pass on the move. A defensive player can be added to guard the wing player. The wing player should break open, positioning her body between the defensive player and the ball. The passer should work to throw a good chest pass to her teammate, breaking open where she can catch the ball and do something with it when she receives it.

ONE-HANDED CHEST PASS

The one-handed chest pass is used a little more today than in the past because many players are picking up the ball right off the dribble with the same hand. This cuts down on the time in which the ball is picked up and passed to a teammate. The passer should throw this pass so that there is good backspin. The hand should come down straight over behind the pass just like a base-ball throw. A good follow-through, similar to that used in shoot-ing, is very important. For practice, use the same drill you would for the two-handed chest pass.

TWO-HANDED BOUNCE PASS

One of the most important passes in the game today is the two-handed bounce pass. It's used quite often to get the basketball from a guard or wing position into a high post or low post when your players are coasting up. This pass is also used quite a bit on the fast break. In throwing the two-handed bounce pass, it is important that you throw the pass so that your teammate will receive the basketball near her waist in a position from which she can take the ball and do something with it. The follow-through for this pass is the same as for the chest pass. Bounce the ball approximately two-thirds of the way between you and your teammate so that the ball will bounce up to your teammate at the waist.

You must be able to throw the bounce and chest passes from both a stationary position and on the move. Most passes in bas-ketball are thrown on the move because players are seldom standing still. In practicing the two-handed bounce pass, use the same drills recommended for the two-handed chest pass. Also practice this pass in a running position. Once you have mastered the ability to throw this pass with two players running up and down the floor, add a third player. One player can dribble, while the other two players spread out on each side. The three players run down the floor passing the ball back and forth with two-handed chest or bounce passes. Once this is mastered with one basketball, add another basketball so that you're using three players and two balls. The middle person must pass one basket-ball back and forth on each of her sides.

Another drill involves throwing the bounce pass in the guard position to the high-post position or center position. A defensive player can be added to the post man or the passer. Now the pas-ser must be more cautious in throwing the pass to the post player. Once mastered with one defensive player, a second defensive player can be added: one on the post player, the other on the passer. The post player now must think about getting herself open. The passer must think about getting into a position to create a good passing angle. She must make a good bounce pass so that the receiver can do something with it.

TWO-HANDED OVER-THE-HEAD PASS

The two-hand over-the-head pass is more difficult than the passes previously described. You've probably seen this pass thrown a lot of times for long distances after a rebound, and used an an outlet pass to begin the fast break. In throwing the two-handed over-the-head pass, the follow-through and fundamentals are basically the same as for the two-handed bounce and two-handed chest passes. Once again, you're stepping to your teammate, throwing the ball with elbows in, palms out, and good follow-through. Do not throw the basketball at the knees or over the head. Throw it so that she can catch it, turn, and face up to the basket, positioned to do something with the basketball immediately.

There are some good drills to be used in connection with this pass. If you have no one to practice with, use a wall. Stand 15 feet away from the wall. Throw the basketball off the wall stressing the fundamentals. Once the pass is mastered at 15 feet, move back to 20 and 25 feet, still throwing the ball properly and stressing the fundamentals. Once this is mastered, draw a square or circle on the wall, and pretend this is your teammate. If you can practice this drill with a teammate, stand anywhere from 20 to 25 feet apart. Pass the ball back and forth stressing the fundamentals.

This pass can also be thrown from an outlet pass position when you rebound. Put one player beneath the basket and another player on the foul line. The player under the basket should throw the basketball against the backboard, jump up, rebound it, and turn to the outside to her teammate's foul line. A good two-handed over-the-head pass should be thrown so that

9. Two-handed over-the-head pass

the player is able to catch the basketball and turn to dribble up the floor. Another drill involves having a player on a line at half court and a player on a line at side court. The player at half court will take the basketball and practice throwing a pass to the player on the side, who is cutting to the basket on the side. This pass should be thrown so that you are practicing hitting a moving target.

ONE-HANDED BASEBALL PASS

Excellent for long distances, the one-handed baseball pass is used more often than the two-handed chest pass, especially since youngsters are better able to throw the ball with one hand than two. This pass should be thrown emphasizing the fundamentals: stepping toward the target, throwing the ball, coming down behind the basketball, getting a good backspin on the ball (just as you do on a baseball), and throwing the ball so that your teammate can catch it in a position to do something with it. Throw this pass with just enough speed—but not too much—to allow your teammate to handle the ball. This pass can be practiced by throwing against a wall, trying to hit a square on the wall that represents your imaginary teammate, or by playing with your teammate, first 20 to 25 feet away from you, throwing the ball back and forth, and gradually moving farther away from each other.

ONE-HANDED HOOK PASS

The one-handed hook pass is used basically to improve passing angles. It involves keeping your body between a teammate and the basketball. You will pivot and hook the pass to your teammate in a position that enables her to do something with the basketball upon receiving it. This pass is frequently used after the player has picked up her dribble and is no longer able to advance the basketball. Many times this pass is thrown from the guard to post position, from the guard to forward position,

10. One-handed baseball pass

or from the forward position into the post. Most of the time you are closely guarded, unable to make a break pass to your teammate. This pass may be thrown as a straight chest pass or as a bounce pass. It is thrown as a bounce pass when you are lower to the floor and it's easier to feed your teammate down low so that she can catch the ball waist high. You can practice this pass with two players passing back and forth. A defensive player can be added to the passer. The passer must then be conscious of using her body between the defensive player and the ball, stepping out to the side, and hooking the basketball to the side of the teammate.

ONE-HANDED BOUNCE PASS

The one-handed bounce pass is more difficult to control than the two-handed bounce pass but takes less time to throw, making it an important factor in today's game. This pass is often thrown from guard to guard, guard to forward, or forward to post. Many times you'll see this pass thrown by the point man on a fast break—a player breaking for the lay-up. This pass is also used on the fast break when you are advancing the basketball rapidly: the middleman picks the ball up right off the dribble with the same hand she has been dribbling with and makes a good bounce pass two-thirds of the way between herself and the receiver. The receiver should be in a position to catch the ball so that something can be done with it immediately. Practice this pass using the same drills outlined for the one-handed and two-handed chest passes.

LOB PASS

The lob pass consists of lobbing the basketball over a defensive player to a teammate for an easy score. This pass is often thrown from the wing position to the post when the defensive player is fronting the player in low post and you are unable to make a straight pass. Throw this pass at a height comparable to rim level or better; your post player will hold off or pin her defensive player until the ball has gone over her head. Then she will release and go catch the basketball. Remember, this is a lob pass, not a hard-throw pass. Many times the pass is thrown from the two-handed over-the-head position since it is easy to control from there.

Drills for practicing this pass include the passer standing in the wing position and the post player posting up in the low post. The passer practices making good two-handed over-the-head lob passes to the basket so that the ball comes down right in front of the basket. The post player catches the basketball and puts it right in the basket. Once you can work on this pass with a passer and receiver, add a defensive player to the post player. Begin by playing the post player in front. Front the post player by just standing still—"dummy defense," as it's called—and throwing the basketball over the defensive player. This will enable the opposite player to catch the basketball and lay it in. Once this is mastered with a dummy defense, tell your defense to go "live." Now practice getting the basketball over the defensive player. Your receiver must be conscious of pinning off your defensive player so she is able to get the basketball. Once this is mastered with one defensive player, add an extra defensive player on the passer. Be especially conscious of making the good pass to your teammate inside, over two defensive players.

The lob pass can also be thrown when the player receiving the pass is on the move, but it is ill advised to teach this to young players. It is a difficult pass to throw and should be thrown only to those players who are big and strong and can hold off their defensive players. Players who are excellent jumpers can capitalize on the lob pass thrown at rim level or above. They can jump up, catch it, and do something with the basketball.

HAND-OFF PASS

The name of this pass describes exactly what occurs. Your teammate comes up behind you and you lay the ball off behind you so that she is able to take it out of your hand and do something with it.

You do not want to take the ball and stick it with force in your teammate's chest or stomach. Just lay the ball out there easily, slipping it to your teammate, allowing her to take the basketball and go hard with it. This pass can be used in the guard-to-guard position, one guard cutting off the other. It may also be employed by the guard dribbling to the wing position and the forward cutting off the guard's rear pass. Additionally it can be used to get the ball back when a guard cuts off a forward on a wing position. Quite often it is used when a pass is made from the guard to the center position; a guard may run a cut to the basket off the center who just hands the basketball right back to the guard cutting in for a lay-up.

Drills for this pass may be practiced in several ways. One can use a guard-to-guard pass, with one guard passing the ball to another guard and then going to get it back. The guard with the basketball would just lay it out there for the guard teammate to cut off and receive the basketball. This pass can be practiced by a guard cutting off a forward to the wing position to regain the basketball. It also can be practiced when a guard dribbles the ball to a wing position and a forward cuts off her rear to receive the basketball back. Another maneuver can be worked on after a guard has passed the ball to her post man making her guard cut. Once mastered, another guard may be added. The two guards scissor off the post man, and the post man now has the option of making the hand-off pass to either guard.

BEHIND-THE-BACK PASS

This pass should not be taught to youngsters because it is very difficult to control and requires mature strength in order for speed to be put on the ball. It should be thrown in a straight line or as a bounce pass and not as a lob pass. Any time you see players throw this pass in a lob—too much in the air—the defensive player can break by and intercept the pass. The behind-the-back

11. Behind-the-back pass

pass should not be thought of as a fancy pass or a "hot dog" pass. It is a pass that should be employed only to create a better offensive situation for a teammate. It may be used to play off on a fast break in which the middleman comes down and fakes one way and throws the pass behind her back to a teammate breaking down the floor for a lay-up. A difficult pass to throw, the behind-the-back pass should never be attempted through traffic, but used exclusively in the open court to sway or force the defensive player in one direction while the player makes the pass in another direction.

Faking 10

Faking is a technique used to deceive an opponent. You appear to move in a direction opposite to the one you are actually going in. Faking is used in the offense when the player has the ball or is trying to get free to receive a pass. Players often practice faking with the ball, but not enough attention is paid to faking without the ball. More time should be spent on such maneuvers because when players are unable to get free the pass is thrown away. The teammate who is about to receive the pass should know how to go about appearing open, so that the pass that is thrown away is not necessarily the passer's fault.

Fakes are normally done with the head, eyes, shoulders, body, feet. All fakes should be done with the elbows in contact with the body so the ball stays within the lines of the body. It is important to keep your balance over the base of your body. If you are off balance when you fake you can easily drop the basketball.

Try to fake without the basketball first. Several types of moves can be made in faking without a ball. Usually you're making a move to get free so you can take possession of the ball. If a fast directional change is required, take a step with one foot, push off it, and take a step in the opposite direction with the other foot. For example, if you're on the wing and a cutter to the top of the key gets the basketball, start your cut toward the basket. Drive hard, playing your right foot against the right side of the basket. Push off shifting your weight, changing it to the left side and your left foot, and then break to the top of the key to receive the pass.

Head and shoulder fakes are also useful. Faking with your eyes, head, and shoulders just to make the defensive player think you're heading in a direction makes even a good defensive player honor your fake and move in that direction.

A player can cut in one direction and quickly change directions. This is called a V-cut. Cut hard four or five steps in one direction, planting your outside foot and cutting back to the inside, and then shifting your weight to your other foot. An advanced player can use a technique that makes her opponent believe she will not be involved in the action. She stays in a relaxed manner, placing her arms to her side and weight on one foot, giving the impression she is just watching the play. As soon as the opponent eases up, the player makes a good, hard cut to receive the pass. If the opponent does not watch the ball, the player may stand nonchalantly with arms down at her side and at the last moment reach up to receive the pass.

Faking with the ball is designed to open passing lanes, free a player for a shot, or even drive toward the basket. To open a passing lane, you can fake with your head, eyes, shoulders, arms, and feet. All fakes are useful if the ball stays in the midline or power line of the body. Don't hold it too far away from your body where you do not have much strength and it can be snapped away. Regardless of the fake, you must use your head and eyes. The defensive player will be watching your head and eyes when you've got the ball in a triple-threat position to find out what you're going to do. Try to fake in one direction and pass to another direction. A player can fake to her left and pass to her right, or she can fake a pass up high and then throw a pass down low. You can fake a pass in one direction and drive in another. Any time you fake in one direction, you're making your opponent move her weight in that direction. When you're faking for a shot or drive there are two things you can do—fake a shot and draw an opponent close so you can drive around, or take a fake and force the player to give ground. If you fake a drive and the defensive player backs up, now you're opened up for a jump shot. It's important that you keep the ball in a triple-threat position. It's a great feeling when you have the option to shoot, pass, or drive with the ball.

You can make a defensive player especially vulnerable when you drive in the direction of her front foot, the foot closest to you. For example, if the defensive player is positioned with her right foot up, that foot will be up against your left side. You can then get open more easily if you fake to your right and drive to your left. I think that whenever you're on offense and are planning a drive, you should focus on the defender's feet. Observe the defender's weight shift and how she balances her weight. This will indicate the direction in which you can clear yourself with the ball.

Moves 11

There are several different types of offensive moves you can employ in a one-on-one set against the defensive player. The main ones include the explode or power move, the jab-and-drive move, the rocker step-and-shoot move, and the cross-over move.

EXPLODE OR POWER MOVE

This move is performed just as its name indicates—you explode to the basket. First, place the ball in a triple-threat position. If the defensive player is on the right side, dribble off with your left hand and take a giant step with your left foot, using your right foot as a pivot foot. Try to get your foot out past the defensive player. Putting the ball out in front of you, protect it with your left leg. Once you have put your leg out so that it's positioned between the defensive player and the ball, push off your right pivot foot. Make sure your head and shoulder are out between the defensive player and the ball. Make a quick move to the basket for the lay-up and get the defensive player on your back.

12. Explode or power move

JAB-AND-DRIVE MOVE

If you're squared up on the defensive player and, for example, you're being favored to your right, pivot with your right foot. Take a short, slow step—a jab step—with your left foot. The defensive player at this point should be relaxed a bit. Now take a quick, powerful move with the left foot and get out past the defensive player. Keep your head, shoulder, and the basketball out past the defensive player. Move quickly to the basket getting the defensive player to your back. If the defensive player favors you to your left, use your left foot as the pivot foot. Make a slow, short step with your right foot. Once the defensive player relaxes, extend your right foot out in a giant step, and, in an explosive move, go quickly to the basket.

Once you have made the slow jab moves and the defensive player does not honor the move but stays close, make your long step and drive to the basket. However, if the defensive player honors your short jab step and backs off, step back into the triple-threat position and shoot your jump shot. For example, if the defensive player guards on the left side, use your left foot as a pivot. Take a slow, innocent, and short step with your right foot. If the move is honored, pull back into the triple-threat position and shoot your jump shot.

The jab step does not always have to be made slowly. Sometimes it can be a quick, hard move. Vary your speed according to the defensive player. Many times a good, hard move will make the defensive player move much more quickly, and this technique is more effective in the jab-and-shoot move. A slow step and then a quick, explosive step is more effective for the jab-and-drive move.

ROCKER STEP-AND-SHOOT MOVE

The rocker move enables you to drive or to shoot your jump shot. If you're being favored by the defensive player on your right side, use your left foot as a pivot and rock back on your right foot. If the defensive player tightens up on you, make the

13. Jab-and-drive move

explode move. If she plays you loose, come back in a triple-threat position and shoot your jump shot. If she plays you on your right, move off in the opposite direction.

CROSS-OVER MOVE

Sometimes you may be cut off by a defensive player, but there's a good move to cope with this. Suppose you are starting to dribble to your right and you're cut off. You should pivot on your left foot and get your body between the ball and the defensive player. Once you have squared up on the defensive player, she'll favor you to one side or the other. You can then use your left foot as a pivot foot and take a short step with your right foot to the defensive player. Try to get your shoulder and head and the basketball out in front of you and make your move toward the basket. Or you can use your left foot as a pivot foot and cross over with your right foot, moving out quickly past the right foot of the defensive player. Again, get your head, shoulder, and the basketball out past the defender and make your quick move to the basket. If the defensive player favors you to the left use your right foot to take a short step and then cross over. Or just make a quick cross over with your left foot, getting it past the left foot of the defensive player.

All of these offensive moves are very important in one-on-one situations and it's very important for you to know what moves you should make. Offensive moves should never be predetermined moves. They should be the moves the defender allows you to make. When you receive the ball, get into a triple-threat position. Read the defense. Understand what the defense is allowing you to do.

If the defense is playing you tight, you automatically know what the best possible move is—a drive. If the defensive player is guarding loosely, look for offensive moves that allow you to shoot your jump shot.

You can also cross up and combine your moves. For example, you can use a rocker move and then a cross over and drive. Or you can use a rocker move and then come back with a jab, drive, or a rocker with a jab-and-shoot move. All these moves become even more effective when they are worked on together. They allow you to gain an edge on an opponent.

DRILLS

There are several drills for moves that you will find valuable. Take the ball out in a triple-threat position. Work on all the offensive moves. Cross them up. Mix them up. Get your own personalized combinations. Also try one-on-one work with a defensive player. You can then expand on this drill by adding a passer who stays in the wing and passes the ball to you at the top of the key. Now just work on your offensive moves. Another drill would be to simulate a one-on-one game-type situation. Get a defensive player to hand the ball to an offensive player who is limited to two or three dribbles before making her offensive moves. This drill is good practice in that it helps to eliminate any excess or wasted dribbling.

Cuts 12

In this "moving without the ball" part of basketball, cuts figure prominently in helping a player get free for a shot. There are four different types of cuts: the front cut, the back cut, the V-cut, and the double cut or scissors cut.

THE FRONT CUT

The front cut is used most of the time by a guard cutting through to the basket. Let's examine a given situation: A guard dribbles down the left side of the floor, then makes a pass to the wing. The guard now starts to make a cut in the opposite direction of the basketball—in this case to the right. After she has made a good, hard cut to the right, two or three steps in deep, she should plant her right foot and push off onto the left foot out between the defensive player and the basketball. At this point, she should cut hard to the basket and look for the return pass.

If the ball is on the right side of the floor, the guard will pass to the wing. She will make a good, hard cut two to three steps to the left, plant her left foot, and push off onto her right foot to the basket. The cut should be made with the right foot between the passer and the defensive player, and she should look for the return pass as she heads to the basket.

THE BACK CUT

The back cut is sometimes called the rear cut. It takes place in two instances. The guard can pass to the wing and make a hard cut with one, two, or even three steps in the direction of the ball. Once the defensive player has come off to cut this off, she plants her outside foot (or foot closest to the ball) and pushes off that foot looking for the return pass.

The back cut is especially effective with a bounce or a lob pass. A second way that it can take place involves a guard coming down and the wing player making a good, hard cut or popping out hard from below the post to the wing position. This maneuver makes the defensive player come out hard to stop her or to guard against her. Once the cutter has moved to the wing position, she plants her outside foot to the sideline and pushes off to the basket. Weight is shifted to the right foot in this instance, and the ball is played to the right side. The cut is to the basket. Look for the pass, usually a bounce pass behind the defensive player.

THE V-CUT

The V-cut can be seen at two or three different places on the floor. When the basketball is in the point position, a spot behind the offensive team's foul line, the wing player starts to cut toward the basket, plants the right foot, and pushes off the left foot, cutting back to the basket. She should attempt to position her body between the basketball and the defensive player. When she receives the basketball, she should get set and shoot a good jump shot. The V-cut from the wing position is a bit different. The cutter starts to move out to the top of the key to receive the basketball. She plants the outside foot closest to the top of the key. Pushing off the opposite foot, she cuts to the basket, looking for the return pass behind the defensive player. It is important in all the cuts that you "read" the defense to be aware of what the defensive player is allowing you to do.

THE DOUBLE CUT OR SCISSORS CUT

When a pass is thrown to the post player, two perimeter players cut simultaneously to the basket off the post player who has the basketball. They cut to the basket seeking a return pass. Usually a guard throws the pass to the post player and makes the first cut in one direction off the post player's opposite side. The guard is looking for a return pass. The other guard crisscrosses off the opposite side of the post player and thus creates a scissors pattern. A guard, a wing, and a post player working together can form a variation of this cut.

DRILLS

Using a cutter and passer in the guard/wing position is one effective drill. The guard dribbles the ball down the left side. She passes to the left wing and cuts to the right. Then she pops back and makes a good guard cut to the basket. This can also be worked on the right side of the floor. The guard comes down. A good pass is made to the wing. The guard cuts to the left, pushes off the left foot, and cuts back to the ball where the basket is for the return pass. When this has been mastered, a defensive player may be added to the cutter. The cutter should strive to make good moves that force the defensive player to go in the direction the cutter desires.

Another variation involves adding a defensive player to the passer and one to the wing, which now creates two situations. The wing player must now work in the open to make a good pass after the guard makes a cut. This can be worked on in the front cut. You can next work on the guard cut with a rear cut.

After the guard makes the pass to the wing player, she must read the defense to determine moves. For example, if the guard comes down on the left side of the floor and passes to the wing and if the defensive player is favoring the inside floor or the right side of the guard cut, the cutter should take one, two, or three steps right at the defender. This will force the defender to shift her weight to the offensive player's right side. A good, hard cut back to the left should now be made to position the offensive player's body between the defensive player and the basket.

Another good drill involves the guard coming down and the wing player popping out to the wing, playing the outside foot and making a quick, back-door cut to the basket, looking for the ball. Once this has been mastered, add a defensive player to the wing cutter and another one to the guard passer. After these drills have been worked on, use a guard and two wings. The guard passes to either wing and runs either a front cut or a rear cut. Or she may come down and pass the ball to the player who has popped out to the wing or hash mark position, planning to run a good back-door cut.

This is also a good situation in which to practice the guard passing the ball to the wing. There you can practice effective guard cutting through to the basket and the opposite player working on the good V-cut. This can involve heading to the basket and cutting to the foul line or faking to the foul line and cutting to the basket for the ball. Once these moves have been learned, add defensive players to the cutter. Then add one to the wing player and create a three-on-three situation for more drill variety and practice.

Offensive Rebounding　　13

Offensive rebounding is probably one of the most overlooked aspects in basketball. Coaches and players spend too much time on perfecting scoring offenses and not enough time on getting performers open for the rebound for the second shot. Regardless of how many offenses you run to get the scoring shot and regardless of how many good shooters you have on your team, you're going to miss some shots. You can't expect to win a basketball game if you think you'll get points with every first shot you take on your offense. Consequently, I feel that a lot more emphasis must be placed on offensive rebounding.

OFFENSIVE REBOUNDING IN THE PERIMETER

There are two areas of the floor we must be concerned with. The first is the perimeter following your shot. The second is in the lane, an area of contact and congestion. Let's first consider the perimeter following your shot. This is an area where many

14. Offensive rebounding in the New York Summer Professional League (July 1980)

players perform poorly. Most players who shoot jump shots nowadays fade away after they release the ball. They head back to the other end, expecting that their ball has gone in. A good offensive rebounder expects every shot to be missed. Without a doubt the best offensive rebounder today is Moses Malone because he goes after every shot and does not stop until the ball comes through the basket. You should assume that every shot will be missed and concentrate on going to the offensive boards after every shot. Do not stop working the offensive rebound until you see the other team has the ball or the ball is in the basket. In offensive rebounding, it is not as important to secure the basketball with both hands as it is to stay after the ball, to keep it "alive." Just one hand on the basketball is enough to tap it away to a teammate or tap it back up against the glass so another teammate can get to it.

In perimeter rebounding, you may not necessarily get rebounds from your own shots. You may come running into the basket because the ball has hit and bounced off the rim, or, after having taken a shot from the perimeter, the ball may have hit the back of the rim and bounced back toward you. There are several different ways in which the ball can come off allowing you the opportunity to get an offensive rebound.

Let's first assume you have taken the shot. Most of the time, the defensive player is going to turn to make contact with you, spreading herself out, arms out to the side, and trying to knock you back with your weight on your heels. This maneuver will make you lean backward away from the basket, depriving you of the momentum needed to head into the basket for your rebound. It is important, therefore, as an offensive rebounder to prevent the defensive player from making contact with your body. If she makes contact, she knows exactly where you are and when you move. She'll then move with you to prevent you from getting around her. When she does try to make contact, stay clear. Make a quick step to the side. If you plan on moving to the left around the defensive player, take a quick, long step with your right foot to the outside of the defensive player's left foot. If you're going to the right of the defensive player, take a quick, long step with your left foot to the outside of the defensive player's right foot. Now your body will be out away from her, but her arm could hold you back. It is important, therefore, to make a quick, hard move straight to the basket, because the defensive player will not be strong enough to hold you off with just her arm. She may try to hook or grab you, which would be a foul on the defensive player. After you've made the quick step away from her, make your move to the basket quickly and under control so that if the ball does hit the basket and bounces up high over your head, you can then stop, go up in the air, and grab the basketball.

You can also get yourself open by allowing some contact with the defensive player in the direction opposite to that in which you plan to make your move. For example, once the defensive player has blocked you out and you plan on moving to the left, touch the right side of the defensive player's body with your right hand. This should not be a holding move, just a touch, enough to let the defensive player feel your contact on that side. This will make her move in that direction. At that point, you make your good, hard move to the left around her arm or right through it.

Another way of getting yourself open is the roll method in which you roll off the contact. If the defensive player makes contact with you, reverse pivot around the defensive player and step in. If you plan on going to the right, step in to the middle of the defensive player's body with your right foot and spin around in a reverse pivot so that your left foot comes around in front of the defensive player's right foot; then, make a good, hard move to the basket.

Offensive rebounding on the perimeter offers a good opportunity to get the rebound and put it back up. Follow your shot, because when you get your offensive rebound, with the defensive player behind you, it should be easy to take the basketball straight to the basket for a lay-up. If there is congestion in the middle, you should be able to go for a quick, short jump shot. Follow straight through to the basket on your next shot because the defensive player who is supposed to be blocking you out is now behind you.

OFFENSIVE REBOUNDING IN THE LANE

The most important area of offensive rebounding is the lane because it is nearest to the basket where most missed shots come off. There are several ways to get yourself open for offensive rebounding in the lane. You can use the methods described in rebounding in the perimeter: cross over with your opposite foot to the opposite side; the roll method; or make contact gently on one side. If you are close to the basket and the defensive player has good rebounding position and has blocked you out, try to keep your hands free from the defensive player. Many times if you put your hands down on the defensive player's body—her back, rear end, or legs—you're apt to be called for a foul if the ball comes off long and you get the rebound. Raise your hands up above your head in case the ball comes off quickly. Now try to walk into the defensive player with your legs, move into her, prevent her from jumping straight up. It is much more difficult for a rebounder to go straight up in the air for a rebound when she has contact from another player. What you are trying to do is walk the defensive player underneath the basket so that she is unable to rebound while you're in a good rebounding position.

Using the cross-over method, you should cross over with your opposite foot and get your body and outside arm free from the defensive player in case the rebound comes off to her side. You're then able to get a hand on the basketball, smack it to a teammate, control the tip back up on the backboard, or try to get the rebound with one hand.

DRILLS

It does not take more than five minutes to work on offensive rebounding every day, and these drills should be worked on daily. They are very important, because—as I said before—it is not likely that you will win many basketball games by the shooting percentage of your first shot down the floor. Regardless of how good your shots are—and I can't emphasize this enough—

15. Offensive rebounding in the lane

you're going to miss almost half and sometimes more. You must, therefore, be able to get yourself open to the basket for rebounding for the second shot.

One good drill is to tap the basketball to the backboard, tossing it up with your left hand and tapping it with your right. We call this drill the 3-in-1 or the 6-in-1. After throwing the ball to the backboard, jump up and control tap it against the backboard three times. On the fourth tap, tap it into the basket. Or control tap it off the board six times and on the seventh time, tap it in. Once this is done with the right hand, move to the left side of the basket and do it with the left hand. It is important to develop the ability to control tap with both hands because you never know which hand is going to be free. If you are unable to control the basketball by tapping it against the backboard with your opposite hand, you're eliminating a great many scoring opportunities in the lane.

Another valuable drill involves throwing the basketball up on the backboard, jumping up, rebounding it strong, coming down with control, and then taking a power lay-up to the basket. Do this on both sides of the basket, or start at the foul line and throw the ball off hard so it comes off deep. Jump up, get the rebound, and now fake the jump shot and make a power move as if you're driving past the defensive player to the basket for another power lay-up.

Try throwing the ball with force off the board from the foul line. The basketball should come off deep. Now run up and get the ball strong, coming down under control. Then go straight back up and shoot the short jump shot. In all these drills, if you miss the shot, go right back for the basketball. Your team should be in the habit of following the basketball regardless of where it is shot from. Many times teams will follow the ball that is shot from the foul line, get the rebound, put it back up and think it's an easy shot. They do not follow the second shot, and if they miss it, the other team will get the rebound.

Another drill, called the "Annie Over," is started with a player on either side of the basket. The first player jumps up and shoots the ball over the basket off the backboard to the other side. The other player jumps up, control taps it back to the other side of the basket off the board. Take turns going back and forth, tapping the ball with control back and forth to each other. Practice for 30 seconds to a minute with the ball being kept off the rim.

The important thing is not to make the shot but to control the basketball so that your teammate can control it when you tap it off the board. This drill can be done with two, three, or four players. With three players, once the first player taps the basketball to the other side, she moves to the inside of the opposite side and gets behind the player there. Rotate yourselves back and forth with the person who taps the basketball, always moving to the inside. This is a good drill because it works on control, and all three players must coordinate. If a fourth player is added, two play on each side and the same amount of rotating is done.

Another drill involves placing an offensive rebounder at the foul line with a defensive player and a coach to shoot the basketball. The coach shoots the ball so that it comes off the basket. The defensive player tries to block out the offensive rebounder who must work to get herself open in order to reach the offensive board for the rebound. A second offensive rebounder and a second defensive player can be added to this drill so that you are playing two-on-two from each side of the lane. Do not rotate until the offensive rebounder has gotten the basketball. You can practice this drill with three-on-three, four-on-four, and even five-on-five. Once you have worked on this drill enough, you will see it pay off in games.

A final excellent drill is called "roller rebounding" or "jungle rebounding." It aids in cutting down on fouls. Place two or three players in the lane with a coach or designated shooter at the foul line. The shooter throws the basketball off the backboard so that it comes off in the lane. The three players are in the lane working for the basketball. Whoever gets the ball is on offense and the other two are on defense. No dribbling is involved. Once you get the basketball, power it straight back to the basket. The defensive players should make some contact with the offensive player to make her, once she gets the rebound, work for the three-point play. This is a good drill to work on early in the year. It forces the player to become aggressive when rebounding and makes her conscious of going to the offensive boards and working against contact and fouls. Once the offensive rebounder gets the ball and makes the shot, the closest player to the net takes the ball and throws it right back to the shooter. The shooter puts it up again and they go after it again. Whoever gets the rebound puts it right back up. If the ball bounces outside the lane, the closest player to the ball runs after it as quickly as possible, grabs the ball, and throws it back to the shooter. The shooter puts it up quickly, and they go after it again.

Dribbling

To dribble or not to dribble—that is the question that makes this part of the game an art. There are certain instances where dribbling must take place. Dribbling should be done by the player trying to get open from a congested area on the floor. Dribbling can initiate a fast break or aid in advancing the ball quickly up the floor. Dribbling should be done to advance the ball against a pressing defense, or to move the ball closer to a teammate, or to try to take the ball in for a lay-up.

You must understand the fundamentals thoroughly in order to become a good dribbler. First, your head should always be up so that you can be aware of where your teammates are when advancing the basketball with a dribble. If you're dribbling with your head down, you are unable to see an open teammate, which can cost you a needed basket. Next, bend at the knees in a comfortable position while you dribble the ball to your side. Dribbling to your side enables you to protect the ball with your body. If it is in front of you, a defensive player will be able to get at the ball. Your feet should be spread, and you should always be on the balls of your feet. Don't be caught flat-footed dribbling the basketball. As a rule, dribble with your right hand, using your left arm to protect the ball. Follow this sequence: bend at the waist, bend the knees, dribble the ball to your side, and use your open hand and arm as a shield in front of you to prevent an opponent from reaching in to take the ball away.

Dribbling resembles shooting because the ball is bounced and controlled with the fingertips and not the palms of the hands. Youngsters should become proficient in dribbling with either hand. This ability can prevent a defensive player from being able to shade or cover you from one side or the other. Ambidextrous dribbling forces an opponent to play you straight up and allows you to go either way.

The following are the various types and styles of dribbles.

SPEED OR HIGH DRIBBLE

The speed or high dribble is usually used when a guard or forward is quickly advancing the basketball from the defensive end to the offensive end, generally for a breakaway lay-up or on a fast break. In such a situation, you want fewer and high dribbles to get the ball up court faster. In a speed dribble, get the basketball out in front of you as far as you can—this is an exception to the rule of dribbling to your side—and act as though you're sprinting to catch up with the ball.

A good drill is to practice dribbling the ball from one end of the court to the other as fast as you can and shoot a lay-up. Or you can have relays with your team. Place half the team on one end of the court and half on the other. Dribble down to the end of the court and come back and toss to the next player. This dribble is not used generally in half court because you are being closely guarded and therefore are more apt to protect the ball.

CONTROL OR LOW DRIBBLE

The control or low dribble is used when a defensive player is guarding you closely. In this case, the fundamentals discussed

16. Speed or high dribble

17. Control or low dribble

earlier must be employed. The ball must be protected with your body, and with your open arm and hand in front of you as a shield against anyone trying to strip you of the ball. The ball is dribbled close to your side so that no one can get at it. Dribble the ball lower to the floor when you are heading to the basket through traffic. In such situations, the ball should never come higher than halfway between the waist and the knee. The higher the basketball is off the floor, the more time the defensive player has to reach in and get it.

A drill for improving this dribble calls for the defensive and offensive players to practice in the jump circle. The offensive player must control the basketball, keeping it away from the defensive player and keeping it as close to her body as possible. The defensive player must try to take the basketball out of the circle without fouling. This makes the offensive player conscious of protecting the basketball with her body and dribbling it as low as possible. Another drill involves lining up three or four players across from one another, close enough so that when a dribbler comes through the line of players to the basket, the defensive player can reach in and try to get a hand on the basketball. The dribbler must therefore be conscious of dribbling the ball low to the floor, controlling the ball, going for a lay-up, and always being aware of the defensive player's threat.

CHANGE-OF-DIRECTION DRIBBLE

The change-of-direction dribble is used when you are being closely guarded and unable to shake free from a defensive player. Dribble in one direction and abruptly change direction, moving away from the defensive player. This enables you to free yourself for an open shot or for a pass to a teammate. The change-of-direction dribble is valuable because it can eliminate a defensive player's snaking in from behind, trying to steal the ball. Changing directions also increases the likelihood of a defensive player fouling the dribbler.

CROSS-OVER DRIBBLE

In the cross-over dribble, start by bringing the basketball up the floor, going to your right. When the defensive player has blocked your advance and you no longer can move in this direction, cross over the dribble in front of you. The basketball goes from your right to your left hand with your body between the defensive player and the basketball. When the defensive player moves to your left to attempt once again to cut you off, cross over in front of her, this time taking the basketball with your left hand and bouncing it hard on the floor quickly in front of you to your right hand. Your body is again between the defensive player and the basketball.

For practice, have a one-on-one drill starting on one baseline and dribbling the basketball up the floor changing directions. In this drill, the defensive player attempts to cut the offensive player off, making her change directions. She then quickly crosses over the basketball from her right to left hand and vice versa, keeping the defensive player from getting a hand on the ball. Relay drills, dribbling from one end line to the other, and changing directions are all helpful drills.

CHANGE-OF-PACE DRIBBLE

In the change-of-pace dribble, you are advancing the basketball up the floor while being closely guarded. If you hesitate just a second, the defensive player will relax, ease up, and drop back on her heels. Once the defensive player stands up and slows down, accelerate as quickly as you can, trying to speed dribble the ball past her so she is unable to defend. A good drill is playing from one end line to the other with the defensive player trying to keep you from advancing the basketball.

BEHIND-THE-BACK DRIBBLE

This dribble should be taught to youngsters only after other dribbles have been mastered. The behind-the-back dribble is

18. Behind-the-back dribble

useful when you are trying to protect the basketball, keeping it away from the defensive player by placing your body between her and the ball. The idea here is to head in one direction. When the defensive player cuts you off so that you can no longer dribble the ball to your side and she is too close for you to cross over in front, the behind-the-back dribble becomes your best tactic.

To form the behind-the-back dribble, overrun the basketball and pass it behind your body to the other side. If you are dribbling with your left hand and want the ball to go behind your back to your right hand, act when your left foot is in the back position and the right foot is forward. Pull the ball back behind your body, bouncing it to the ground, trying to lead, and throw a lead pass to yourself. Push the basketball out in front of your body so that your momentum is not slowed down. If you are dribbling with your right hand, pull the ball back behind you when your left foot is forward, your right foot back, and you have overrun the ball. You then make another quick about pass, leading yourself to your left hand so that you maintain your speed. This dribble is very difficult. The other dribbles discussed are more important in technique and should be used to teach youngsters the art of dribbling.

REVERSE DRIBBLE

The reverse dribble involves changing directions while keeping your body between the defensive player and the ball. For example, pivot on your left foot. Pull the basketball back, being careful not to turn the ball over and reverse in the opposite direction. Step with your right foot and fling the ball around, keeping your body between the ball and the defensive player. Or, pivot with your right foot. Step back around with your back to the defensive player on your left foot and fling the basketball from your left to your right hand. Be careful not to let the basketball get away from your body. Keep it as close as you can. To practice, dribble from one end line to the other. Go to your right, reverse back to your left, reverse back to your right, and so on.

SPIN DRIBBLE

The spin dribble, also called the whirl dribble, is similar to the reverse dribble except that the spin dribble is much quicker and the basketball never changes hands. It remains in the same hand the whole time.

BACKWARD DRIBBLE

This move involves dribbling the basketball while backing up all the time. Be conscious of keeping the basketball down low and controlling it. The ball should be kept more to your front, since you do not know what's behind you. If you are backing up with the ball at your side, you may not be aware of a defensive player sneaking up and stealing the ball. But if the ball is controlled in front of you and you are backing up very slowly, you are able to protect it from any defensive player moving up behind you. At the same time you are aware of the defensive player in front of you. This dribble may be used when there is a loose ball in the court and a player snatches it and pulls it back toward her body, backing away from the area of congestion.

BETWEEN-THE-LEGS DRIBBLE

This dribble is similar to the behind-the-back dribble. Dribble the basketball to your side. If you are dribbling with your left hand, your right foot is forward and your left foot back. Push the basketball between your legs down to the floor so that it bounces up to your side in your right hand. If you are going forward, you're able to explode quickly with the ball because the defensive player will be on the left side. If you're dribbling the ball with your right hand, push it from your right side quickly through your legs to your left side when your left foot is in the forward position and your right foot is back. If you're going to back up, take the ball through your legs from one hand to the other. Pull back, away from the defensive player. This dribble is

19. Between-the-legs dribble

most useful in a congested area where quick control is needed to get the ball from a defensive player and move out from the contact area swiftly.

DRILLS

Chairs are convenient props for practicing dribbles. Place them on various spots on the floor to simulate defensive players. Arrange the chairs in "figure eights" or in back-to-back pairs with just a bit of dribbling space between. For example, dribble up to two chairs and change direction, moving away from them; practice the cross-over dribble or the behind-the-back, reverse, spin, and between-the-legs dribbles. You can dribble in place, keeping the ball low, and practice crossing over the basketball, going behind the back, between the legs, backing up with the ball, and accelerating with it. Play a game of tag with every participant dribbling a basketball. The person designated as "it" must dribble the basketball while trying to touch other participants in the game. Once tagged, the player must leave the playing area. Such a drill heightens awareness of using all kinds of dribbles in different areas of the floor. Speed and control can be developed through such drills.

Ball Handling Drills   15

The drills in this chapter are ones that can be worked on to improve ball handling, speed, and general feel for the basketball.

I think it's important to wake up the hands. Take the basketball and pound it in each hand as hard as you can. Let your hands get a good "feel" for the basketball. Squeeze the ball. Put it between your hands with your arms spread above your head and squeeze it as quickly as you can with your fingertips. Bounce the ball up in the air as quickly as you can, keeping your arms straight. Do this with your right hand and then your left. The idea is to keep the ball on your fingertips and not let it touch your palms. Another way of getting the feel of the basketball is by tapping the ball from one hand to the other as quickly as you can, using your fingertips and keeping your arms straight above your head. Your hands should be about six inches apart. Bring the ball down in front of your body all the way to your knees and then take it back up while continuously tapping the ball with your fingertips. This will build up your touch and strengthen your fingers.

To get the feel of the basketball and work on ball handling, practice the around-the-body drill. Put your legs together and pass the ball around your body in a circular motion as quickly as you can. Move the basketball around your legs, waist, head. Reverse the motion and keep at it until you can do it very rapidly, getting the feel of the ball without dropping it or losing control.

Another drill involves spreading your legs and passing the ball in a circle around your right leg as fast as you can and then around your left. Once mastered, this drill can be expanded into the figure eight drill where the ball is passed through your legs in a figure eight motion while keeping your knees bent, with your legs spread apart and your waist bent. Keep your head up, looking straight ahead.

To improve dribbling ability, practice the circular dribble around your left leg. Spread your legs the way you did when you passed the ball around them. Dribble the basketball in small circles around your left leg and your right leg. Then proceed to the figure eight drill. Bend over on your toes with the ball at your feet, your knees and waist bent, and your head straight ahead. Instead of looking at the ball, be conscious of looking for the open player. At the same time dribble the basketball in a figure eight motion through your legs. Once you have mastered this technique, dribble twice with your left hand, three times with your right hand, going two dribbles through your legs on your left side and three dribbles through your legs on your right side. Reverse the procedure.

Another dribbling drill involves getting in a good fundamental stance. Dribble the ball low to your right, next to your body. Keep your eyes closed. Practice dribbling the ball through your legs, behind your back, crossing over to the other hand, sitting down while you're still dribbling, laying down on the floor, sitting back up, standing up. Do any kind of movement you can while retaining control of the ball and not losing the dribble. Do not look at the ball.

The spider drill is another good practice procedure. Bend your knees, dribble the ball to the same spot between your legs, once with your left hand and once with your right. Put your hands behind you quickly and dribble once to your left, once to your right. Bring your hands back to the front hitting the ball quickly with your left hand, then to your right hand, then to the back again with your left and right hand. Dribble with your fingertips. Bounce the ball in the same spot every time.

Yet another drill involves standing straight up with the legs spread. Slam the ball between your legs. Move your hands behind you and try to catch the basketball.

To increase hand quickness, practice this drill. Throw the ball in the air and clap your hands as many times as you can before catching it. You should be able to clap 10 to 30 times, depending on how high you throw the ball. For a variation, try to catch the ball behind your body by positioning your hands behind your waist.

Next you can try holding the ball straight out in front of you with two hands. Drop it straight to the floor and try to clap your hands behind you before the ball hits the ground. As a variation, drop the ball in front of you and clap your hands behind and in front of your body, attempting to catch the ball before it hits the ground. Try to keep increasing the number of claps that you average before you catch the ball.

For another drill, hold the basketball at your waist. Drop the ball in front of you. Clap your hands behind your back and touch the ball before it hits the ground. If you are working with a teammate, let her stand behind you with the ball, holding it with one hand against the back of your neck. You stand with your hands on your waist. When your teammate releases the ball, clap your hands as quickly as you can in front of you and attempt to catch the ball behind you before it hits the ground.

Once these drills have been mastered, practice by yourself holding the ball at the back of your knees. Bend over, drop the basketball to the floor, clap your hands quickly, and catch the ball before it hits the floor.

These exercises are all difficult and time consuming. But you must be willing to put the time and effort into them if you wish to master them and become a proficient basketball player.

Screening 16

Screens used intelligently aid offenses. They can help a teammate who is ready to shoot at the basket by providing her with a human shield. They can give the ball to a shooter who comes up behind them. In setting up a screen, you must give the opponent one step if she is unable to see the screen forming. The one step doesn't have to be allowed if your opponent can see you setting up the screen. Spread your legs and keep them steady so that you won't be knocked off balance. Keep your arms stationary and use them for protection by holding them out. If you've set up a side screen, set your body so that your opponent's leg is positioned between your legs. If you set a side screen and your teammate takes the ball and starts to drive, keep your eye on the basketball. Turn your foot closest to the basket and use this as a pivot. Move your body in a roll to the basket. Never turn your back on the basketball for your teammate might have to pass the ball to you.

20. Screening

Part Three

DEFENSIVE SKILLS

Defense is the part of the game that everyone enjoys the most and loves to see. Defense is also a very important part of winning. Lots of teams can score points. But the team that can not only score points but also stop the other team from scoring is the team that will win consistently. Therefore, defense is the part of the game on which you should spend most of your time.

Offense comes naturally to athletes, and I think athletes are so much better today than they were years ago. Their natural athletic ability will allow them to score points. But defense skills must be worked on as a team concept. Good team defense is essential for a winning basketball team. If you read of John Smith scoring 35 points, the natural question is: Who was guarding John Smith? It is not one man's responsibility to stop somebody. It is the team's responsibility. Many times a player leaves the opponent she is assigned to in order to help out in another situation, and the ball comes back to that opponent who then scores. This is not an individual player's fault but rather the team's failure to work as a defensive unit.

Body Position 17

Proper body position is essential for the good defensive player. Some people say you play defense with your feet and your heart. Well, I think you play defense with your feet and your brains. Your brains tell you what to do, and a good defensive player is a smart basketball player. She knows what to do and exactly when to do it. She knows that the different parts of the body all play a role in defense. Her feet are spread in a comfortable manner. Years ago people said the feet should be spread way out, but if your feet are spread out too far, you can't move quickly. The name of the game in defense is quickness. You've got to beat the offensive player to a particular spot on the floor. Your feet should be comfortably spread apart, a distance of about shoulder width.

The good defensive player plays on the balls of her feet, keeping herself up, anticipating the next move. Being ready to move quickly, you should play defense in a toe-to-heel manner. It does not matter which foot is back, but one foot should be a little behind the other. Your toes should be pointed straight ahead with the toes of the back foot parallel to the heel of the forward foot. If you are going to slide on the floor from one side to the other, keep your feet in a parallel position. Stay on the balls of your feet and slide quickly. Most of the time, though, you will not be sliding but making a forward and backward movement. The best position, therefore, is the toe-to-heel stance.

The good defensive player keeps her knees bent, flexed, and loose. You can't move fast if your knees are tight. Her waist is bent but her back is straight. Years ago, defense experts said to play defense as though you are sitting down. I disagree because such a position is not comfortable. Bending the knees and bending the waist while keeping the back straight can be done comfortably. A straight back enables you to see the floor.

MOVEMENTS FOR ARMS, HANDS, AND FEET

It is important to keep your arms and hands moving as much as possible in the passing lane. The idea is to make the offensive player be as careful as possible in making passes. Hopefully, with your hand in the passing lane, you will be able to knock down a pass. Or you may be able to stop an opponent from moving. While harassing the opponent with hand movements is a good tactic, you should avoid hitting or tapping down toward the ball because that creates fouls. Instead, swing in an upward motion from floor to head in a move to knock the ball away from an opponent. Talk as much as possible when playing defense. Keep your teammates aware of what you are doing on the court at all times. You can yell out: "Help!" "Stop the ball!" "Watch the high-post player!" and so on.

There are two types of slides. One is the cross-over slide where your feet cross over and you're almost running to beat your opponent to a spot on the floor. When using the other type of slide, your feet do not cross.

DRILLS

Drills can help improve defensive maneuvers. A player can stand in a defensive position and use the stutter step as rapidly as possible. Remember to keep feet parallel to the floor. The team can also spread out on the court in defensive position. The coach checks each player making sure that feet, arms, hands, and head are all in the proper defensive position. The players spread out on the half court with their backs to the basket as though they are playing defense. The leader faces them. She points or slides in a certain direction, and the players must slide in that direction. Practice footwork for 30 seconds, then rest for 30 seconds and repeat the process five or ten times. It is important to stay fresh when playing defense. If you are tired, you will have a tendency to stand up and slow down.

Another drill involves one defensive player, one offensive player, and no ball. The offensive player moves around the floor as if she's trying to get open to receive a pass. The defensive player is in good defensive stance, with her hands behind her back. She then moves and works on footwork, staying behind the offensive player. In another drill the offensive player has the basketball. Starting on one end line, the offensive player takes short zigzag cuts, dribbling the ball down the floor. The defensive player, with hands behind her back, must get over and cut the offensive player off, making her turn in the opposite direction. Once she turns, the defensive player must again run over with zigzag or slide movements, cut her off, and make her change directions.

GENERAL PRINCIPLES

When someone on your team takes a shot and misses and the other team retrieves the ball, you are on defense. Then, you must do one of two things. If you are playing full court defense, you must locate the opponent you have been assigned to guard and get good defensive position on her all the way down the floor. If you're playing half court defense, get back to the other end as quickly as you can, always keeping an eye on the ball and your opponent at the same time.

Always position yourself to see both the ball and the opponent. Never be just a ball watcher. While you're watching the ball, your opponent could be moving away from you. As a defensive player you must force the ball to the middle of the floor as much as possible. Take the outside position so that the offensive player has no choice but to go back to the middle of the floor where you have help from your teammates.

A defensive player should always stay to the side of her opponent. This means the player is generally closer to the ball than her opponent. If the ball is to her opponent's left, the defensive player must also be to the left. She should overplay her opponent, trying to keep the basketball away from her as much as possible. Denying the ball to the offensive player is of prime importance.

When playing defense, always face the ball. Try not to turn your back on the ball even when you're running or cutting off the player you are guarding. Position yourself toward the sideline so that the offensive player cannot drive by you. Confront an opponent who cuts across a lane to the basket. If the ball is on the right and you're guarding on the left side of the floor, you should be off the woman you are guarding in the direction of the basketball. If she cuts across the lane to the basket, you must now get up in front of her to prevent her from receiving a direct pass. The defensive player should be ready to assist any teammate when necessary if her opponent does not have the ball. She should be ready to help defend against a dribbler who is free or a cutter who has gotten away from her opponent. If she is on the weak side, she is primarily responsible for helping her teammate against lob passes or any type of back-door cut.

Guarding
the Player
without the Ball   18

When you are on defense, you will find that 90 percent of the time the player you are guarding does not have the ball. Knowing how to guard such a player is therefore very important. If your opponent is one pass away from the ball, you must be in the overplay position. You should be up with your front leg, arm, and shoulder, and your head in the passing lane. Keep your arm extended facing the ball, so you will be able to knock down the passing cut. Use your peripheral vision to keep an eye on the opponent who has the ball and your own opponent at the same time. You should be able to look straight ahead and see one player on one side and the other player on the other side without having to move your head. When your opponent moves, trying to get open, shuffle your feet. Don't let the opponent evade you. Stay as close as possible, about one arm's length away.

If you are guarding an offensive player who is two passes away from the basketball, you should be off the offensive player you are guarding, two steps away from the ball in an open position so that you can see the rest of the court. If you are guarding the opposite guard in the backcourt and you are one pass away, you would play a little differently than you would when the ball is in the front and you are playing one pass away from the wing. When you are playing out front as the opposite guard, take one step away from the woman you're defending against and move in the direction of the basketball to the middle of the floor. It is your responsibility to stop the dribble if she should get by your teammate and move to the middle of the floor. Make the dribbler back away, unable to penetrate to the basket. It is your responsibility to stop any pass and slow it to the middle of the floor because by now you should be in the middle of the floor in the passing lane with your hands moving. Make sure the offensive player you are assigned to does not cut between you and the basketball. Each time she tries to make a cut to the ball, make her cut behind you. Be ready when the ball is passed back to the player you're defending against. Quickly get back to the outside of the floor in a good defensive position to stop the penetration of the pass on the ground.

DEFENSE AGAINST THE WING OR CORNER: ONE PASS AWAY

If the offensive player you are guarding is unable to get the basketball in the area where her team starts the offense—usually in the foul line extension—she will most likely make a hard cut to the basket. It is crucial that you stay with your opponent. There are two ways of doing this. First, if the opponent makes a back-door cut, open up to the ball quickly, then retreat to the basket. Pivot with your foot closest to the basket, opening your body to the ball and sliding back with your player so that she does not get away from you. If she is unable to get the ball, she will come back out again and you can close down again. Depend on your outside foot. Close down your body in a position between the ball and your opponent. Second, don't open to the ball but stay down all the way if your opponent makes a back-door cut. Maintain a position that enables you to see the ball. If your opponent is in the corner, she is really cutting down the floor. She is only able to move along the baseline or the middle of the floor. If you're guarding a player in the corner one pass

21. Defending against the wing or corner: one pass away

away, play off one step in the direction of the ball. Step back, keeping the ball and player in full view. If your opponent begins to penetrate between you and a teammate, move in front of the ball and eliminate penetration. Give your teammate time to get back and cover and then get in a good defensive position and overplay your opponent. Always shade the baseline when your opponent receives the ball in the corner. Eliminate penetration. Force the offensive player to take the ball back to the middle of the floor where you have help.

Drills

There are some very appropriate drills for the player who is one pass away from the ball. In groups of four—either two guards and their opponents or a player and a wing and their opponents—pass the ball from guard to guard or player and wing, slowly increasing speed so that all the players can master getting into the correct defensive positions. In a variation of the drill the ball handler drives to the basket between two defenders, who must attempt to cut off the offensive player. Another drill involves the opposite guard. A cut is made to the basket and the help side guard must stop the offensive player from making the cut between the basketball and herself. This drill can be run with two guards or one guard and one wing.

DEFENSE AGAINST THE WING OR CORNER: TWO PASSES AWAY

If the ball is two passes from the player you're assigned to on the wing, that ball must be on the opposite side of the floor. Take two steps off in the direction of the basket. You can then see the player with the ball and the player you're assigned to guard. When the pass is returned and is now one pass away move into the overplay position. Back away. Get off two steps from your opponent in an open position. This weak side defense is very important since you must be ready and in position to see the entire floor and help when a back door comes outside.

Drills

A variety of drills exist for the defensive player who is two passes away. The first drill can use two guards, an opponent, and one wing. The guard on the same side of the court as the wing starts with the ball and passes to the other guard off the wing. At first, the three other players should remain stationary while the defense, positioned two passes away from the ball, becomes accustomed to the movements of the ball. After you've done this a few times, you can vary the drill by moving to the other side of the court and having the offensive players play defense and the defensive players play offense. Vary the speed of the drill until you approximate game condition speed.

Another drill involves five offensive and five defensive players. The coach tells an offensive player where to make a pass. The emphasis should be on defensive positioning of players in this drill. Once they get accustomed to the movements, the tempo of the passes can be speeded up. Another drill involves a group of three—a wing with the ball, an offside wing player, and her defender. Practice the flash pivot where the offensive player on the opposite side of the floor cuts to the basket. The defensive player on the weak side should practice attempting to cut her off from the basket.

Guarding the Player with the Ball 19

An offensive player with the basketball can drive, pass, and shoot. You must be in a position to prevent her from doing these things. Always "shade" an offensive player, forcing her to the middle of the floor where you have help. Keep your hands and arms moving and your head up on the basketball as it is being dribbled. Stay within arm's length to prevent her from driving by you. If the offensive player pulls up to shoot the basketball, step in between her legs with your foot. Put your hand in her face. Don't hit her, but put your hand 12 to 18 inches away from her face in order to distract her. Then you can attempt to block the shot.

DEFENDING AGAINST A PASS AND CUT

From the guard position with a defensive player and two guards, the defensive player should harass the offensive player, making her pick up the dribble. Once she has passed to the opposite guard, the defensive player must get out quickly in the direction of the ball. She must strive to keep the basketball and

22. Defending against a pass and cut

the opponent she is trying to guard in front of her. Emphasis should be on quick movement.

In practice, she should work on the guard she's assigned to defend, cutting to the basket or the basketball. She must get out in front of the cutter, making her cut behind the defensive player to the basket. When this drill is mastered with one defensive player, a second should be added. Playing two-on-two, the same drill should be worked on. Once it is done from the guard position, it should be practiced from the guard and wing position. Place the defensive player on the guard with the basketball. Make the guard pick up the basketball. Get the offensive player to pass to the wing position. Now move quickly in the direction of the basketball, opening up your body so you can see the player with the basketball and the player you're assigned to defend. After working on the quick movement there, have the offensive player you're assigned to make a cut to the basket or the basketball. You must now try to make the offensive player cut behind you by cutting in front. After working on this, add another defensive player to the wing position and work two-on-two.

When a pass is thrown into the pivot, honor the move of the offensive guard toward the post player. When the actual cut is made, get in front of the cutting player and head her off. If you are defending in the pivot from behind the post player, keep your head up watching for movement. When the scissors guard cuts, leave the post player and help out by defending against the guard who has gotten the return pass and is poised to shoot.

DEFENDING AGAINST THE SHOOTER

There should never be a time when you're guarding a player on a drive and your feet leave the floor while you are attempting to block a shot. Doing so allows the offensive player to take you up in the air and drive around you or drive and make contact. This sets up the possibility of a foul and a three-point play. When you are in good defensive position on the basketball and when the offensive player takes the basketball up to shoot, move your feet quickly. Step in between the offensive player's legs using the foot closest to her. Put the hand closest to her in the area of her face in order to harass and distract her. Now pivot around on the foot you have stepped on and get the shooter on your back. Try to make contact with your rear end against the shooter's thighs. This knocks the shooter back on her heels and does not allow her to get momentum going for the offensive rebound. Spread your arms and legs out to the side. If the shooter does make a move to the basket, you will feel it. You can then move your body in front of her to keep her from the basket.

If you are defending against a shooter in the lane in the post, be certain to establish your position. If possible, keep your feet

23. Defending against the shooter

on the ground. This is difficult, but the only players who can afford not to are the bigger players who know how to go about shot blocking. It is important that you step into the shooter but try not to make contact because the officials are looking out for that all the time. You may want to put both hands over your head. This makes it difficult for the shooter to see the basket, especially if she is smaller than you. Do not lean over her or put your arms over her head because she is entitled to this territory. Should she jump up straight into your arms, you will be called for a foul.

DEFENDING AGAINST THE DRIBBLER

For this type of defense, maintain good body position with your head up on the ball. If the dribbler is moving to the right, get over, head up on the basketball so that the offensive player must stop and change directions since she is unable to get around you. As soon as she crosses the ball over to the opposite side, get over quickly to that side, head up on the basketball. If you are head up on the ball, you are in good defensive position and the offensive player will be going nowhere. Know how fast your opponent is. If she's quicker than you are, play a little looser to eliminate the possibility of her driving past you. If you are quicker than she, then play tighter on the basketball to harass her. As a general rule, it is best to play loose early in the game until you determine your opponent's speed. Then as the game progresses, get closer to your opponent to the point where you feel sure that she will not penetrate past you.

A safe rule to follow when you are not familiar with an opponent's speed is to play one and a half arm's length away from her. An arm's length is playing very close.

Drills

Pair up a defensive and offensive player. The offensive player starts at the end of the court and dribbles toward the opposite basket. The defensive player must try to turn the offensive player

24. Defending against the dribbler

as much as possible by getting over in front of the ball. Once the offensive player turns in the opposite direction, the defensive player must quickly get over to that side and try to turn the offensive player back.

In another drill, the offensive player can try to get by the defensive player. If she does, she can go for the lay-up. The defensive player can try to get back as quickly as she can. This can be done two-on-two in the same fashion. Your head should be directly in front of the ball where your opponent is dribbling. The weak side defensive player should concentrate on body position. She should try to get over between the two offensive players ready to help in case of penetration. She must be able to maintain a position where she can see both the offensive player with the ball and the player she's assigned to guard.

A drill involving the dribbler in either corner position has the dribbler attempt to ride the baseline. The defensive player must work on proper footwork and get over and cut off the baseline, thereby forcing her opponent back to the middle of the floor. Another drill is to make a dribbler anywhere on the court change directions as many times as possible. The defensive player must get over in front of her as quickly as possible. A good one-on-one drill requires the defender to use only footwork to get over as close as she can to make her opponent turn. Or, the offensive player can cross in front of the defensive player and the latter tries to get a hand on the basketball. In such a case, never slap down from head to toe, but swing up from floor to head in order to get the bottom of the basketball.

Guarding
a Player
on the Fast Break 20

In a one-on-one situation, where the offensive player is trying to break away, the defensive player must get back to the basket as fast as she can. She must get set in defensive position in the middle of the lane and try to beat the offensive player down the floor. Once the offensive player gets down the floor and starts to move to the basket, the defensive player must get over in front of her and establish position before she gets there. Either the offensive player will see the defensive player in her path and will hold up, giving the defensive player's teammates time to get back, or she will be out of control and charge into the defensive player causing an offensive foul. It is worth stressing the importance of getting to the basket quickly and establishing position in the lane. If you do not get to the basket in time and are in a position where you are running side by side with the offensive player, do not foul or let your feet leave the ground. Instead, try to prevent the shot by getting your hands up in front of it and maintain head and body position to facilitate rebounding should the shot be missed. I have noticed that many times the offensive player shoots out of control and misses, but the defensive player is not in good position and therefore does not get the rebound.

Guarding
the Post Player 21

This is one of the most important parts of the game because games are won and lost inside the lane. Different defensive areas include the high post, the medium post, and the low post.

In the high post, always stay between the basketball and the player you're assigned to defend. If the basketball is out front in the guard position, as a defensive player you should play in a semifront position. Place one leg, your head, shoulder, and arm in front of or to the side of the offensive player in the passing lane. Try to eliminate any direct pass straight into the post. Your other hand and leg should be behind the offensive player. Every now and then make contact with your body so that you know where she is at all times. If she starts to make a move and roll away from you to the basket, you will feel the contact with your back hand and can make the adjustment.

DEFENSIVE PLAY IN THE HIGH POST

There are three ways to guard a player in the high-post position. One involves your stepping quickly in front of the offen-

25. Guarding the post player

sive player and then swinging back to the other side again in the passing lane on the opposite side of the player. Or you may cross quickly behind, depending on how dangerous the offensive player is. If she is an excellent scorer and a factor in the offense, step in front and try to eliminate any passing to the post. If, however, she is not a very good offensive player and a pass to the post will not be as dangerous, then you can step behind the offensive player and get to the other side. But do so quickly in a 1-2-3-step move. Keep getting your hand in the passing lane to prevent any pass from going in there.

A second way of defending the high post is to play straight behind. Guard the offensive player, but allow the ball to come into the post. Once the ball passes into the post, play the offensive player straight up to the basket because she will be likely to try to get the ball in the triple-threat position. Playing behind is usually done when the offensive player is not too threatening or when the wings like to run a lot of back doors. Taking passes from the guards, the post player may play behind, enabling her to get off and help in a back-door cut more easily.

The third way to defend the high post would be to front the high-post player completely. Play in front with your back against the offensive player, facing the ball. Keep one arm down around you, and, barely touching now and then, make enough contact to always know where the offensive player is. If she moves away from you to the basket, you will know it because of the lack of contact and you can look up quickly and find her. This maneuver is used in high post only against top offensive threats. It is used more frequently in low post.

DEFENSIVE PLAY IN THE MEDIUM POST

There are three styles of defensive play in the medium post: semifront, in which you play to the side with arm, head, and front leg in the passing lane; playing behind, which is dangerous because the offensive player is close to the basket and you may wind up allowing the pass to go into the lane too easily; and fronting completely, which attempts to deny the post player the ball.

Playing to the side is generally the best defensive procedure. The rule here is to determine on which side of the offensive player you should position yourself. For example, if the basketball is above the foul line extension—and this would be in wing position out and toward the backcourt—play the offensive player in the post between the ball. This means you'll be playing in the high-post side. Your hand, head, shoulder, and leg should be in the passing lane. Once the ball is passed to below the foul line, step over in front. Now you have to get to the opposite side to play the low-post side. Remember always cross over in front of the offensive player because if you go behind, you allow the pass to be made in the medium post. Step in a 1-2-3 fashion, and you're now playing defensive semifront to the side on the low-post side. Again, you may play behind but I don't advise it for that allows the basketball to come in. If you should front here, it is highly important to get your back as close as possible to the front of the offensive player. This enables you to feel contact. You can increase this contact by putting your hand behind you every now and then and touching the offensive player. Raise your other hand up above your head to protect against lob passes.

DEFENSIVE PLAY IN THE LOW POST

Defense in the low post is very similar to that in the medium post. If the ball is above the wing, play on the high-post side or the medium-post side. If the ball is below the foul line or goes to the corner, cross over in front. Don't let the ball come into the post. Be conscious of the lob pass. Get in the low-post side in a semifront prepared to cut off the baseline side. If the offensive player does get the ball, square up straight behind her. Don't allow her to get to the baseline. Make her move into the middle of the floor where you have plenty of defensive help. On some occasions a team will play with two post players. In this case, you must know how to defend against the weak side post player. Use the same basic rules we talked about previously. Get off in the position of the ball and the player you're assigned to defend. Be ready to cut off your opponent when she cuts to the basketball. Chances are there will be a screen coming that you will need to get over; go around the screen as quickly as you can. Head the offensive player off when she tries to cut for the ball. Don't let the pass be made to the post player, or at least make your opposition work for it so that it's a tough pass.

DRILLS

Post defense play has a variety of drills. Work on the high post with two guards and a post player. Place one defensive player on the post player. Pass the ball back and forth from guard to guard. The defensive player must adjust to where the ball is on the floor. Quick movements, getting around the defensive player in the post, and defending against the pass must all be worked on.

Another drill utilizes a guard and wing player. The high-post person plays at the front of the foul lane. The defensive player must work on getting around quickly from one side to the other to prevent the pass into the post. Work on foot movement and on lobbing the pass into the post with the defender attempting to stop the pass. Medium-post drills can be practiced with a guard and wing doing the same drill. Or you can work a wing and corner player in the medium post.

Another useful drill in the low post is to have a wing and corner player. The defensive player must now work to get around the offensive player or work in front, whichever defensive technique she wishes. A drill with the basketball on the wing is to have just a passer and defensive player in the low post. The offensive player works hard to get open in the low post. The defender must try to block the pass coming in. Once the pass does come in, the two players can engage in a one-on-one game.

Another drill would involve movement on offense from high to low to medium post. Station four players on the perimeter as passers—two guards and two forwards. The offensive post players should move to the ball, and the defender should attempt to deny the ball to her. This drill will make a defensive player aware of fronting, staying in the passing lane, and cutting the player off if she gets to the ball.

Defensive Rebounding 22

No offensive team wins games by making their first shot all the time. And that's why defensive rebounding is such a major part of the game of basketball today. A team that allows its opponents the opportunity to get a second, third, and fourth shot at the basket is a team that loses games. That's why you must work every day on defensive rebounding and blocking out.

Each player has a responsibility in this area. Each player must make contact, block out, and keep opponents out of the lane. Whenever a shot goes up, step in, make contact with your opponent, and pivot. Get her on your back, extending your arms so that any way she moves you can move with her and keep her on your back. It is important to hold her out for a count of 1000, 1001, 1002. This allows enough time for the inside players to get to the boards. The ball will be coming off after that period of time. Don't just turn and go out for the ball, for your offensive opponent has an equal opportunity to grab the ball. Get your opponent behind you so that you are between her and the basketball at all times.

Guards should block and keep their opponents out of the foul lanes as much as possible. When the ball goes up, the guard

26. Defensive rebounding

should make contact on her opponent and not allow the boards to be crashed. Many times inside players work strenuously to keep their opponents off the boards but guards have a break down and don't block out. Then you'll see an offensive guard come racing through for a rebound and an easy lay-up. Guards should break out to the foul line for the outlet pass for the fast break once they notice their team has possession of the ball.

Forwards playing the forward or wing position must stay between the offensive player and the basketball at all times. The offensive player should be on your back. Know where she is so that she can't get by you and crash the boards. Don't give her room to jump, but at the same time look for the long rebound and be ready to jump for it. Keep your opponent out of the lane since enough is going on there without her presence.

Post players should stay between the basketball and their opponent. They should keep contact with their opponent on their back. Make contact with your rear; use your thighs to knock your opponent's momentum backward. It is very tough for a player to jump effectively when going backward. Lean on her. When you hold her off—count 1000, 1001, 1002, 1003—and when you see the ball coming off, go get it. Grab the ball at its peak. Work on your timing. When you go up, spread yourself out and take up as much room as possible. Get your legs spread out, your arms straight, and both hands ready to grab the ball tightly. Don't attempt to be a superstar and stab the ball with one hand. You may lose control. When you return to the floor, keep the ball moving for this can help you draw a foul. Never bring the ball straight down and give an opponent the chance to slap the ball out of your hands. Keep the ball above your head and look for a good outlet pass.

DRILLS

Position a player with the ball about 5 feet from the hoop and throw the basketball against the backboard. Get the player to go after the ball concentrating on rebounding fundamentals. A variation for two players involves one shooting from the foul line and the other practicing making contact while going up for the ball. You can also have two defensive and two offensive players and a coach. The two defenders should make contact with their opponents and go for the ball.

Another drill involves two wings and a pivot player and their opponents. An offensive player should shoot the ball. The other players should work on blocking out, with one designated to get the basketball. You can add players, creating four-on-four and five-on-five situations. When using the maximum number of players— the five-on-five—stress the execution of the effective outlet pass. Remember, this pass should be thrown over the head with two hands or as a baseball pass, and the ball should never be brought down into traffic.

Defense
Against Screening 23

Screens are valuable weapons for the offense and frustrate defensive players who have not been trained in how to cope with them. Many games are won and lost as a result of how effectively players and teams cope with screens. There are basically three ways to defend against screens: sliding over the top of the screen between your opponent and the screener; sliding behind the screen, that is, going between the screen and your teammate who is defending against the screener; and switching opponents, where your teammate picks up the player you're defending and you defend against the screener. This tactic should be called out only by the player defending against the screen. She should call out "screen left" or some other message to point out the screen's location.

In the guard-to-guard situation in the backcourt, you must know your opponent's effective shooting range. If a side screen is set and your opponent is not in good scoring range, slide behind the screen. Your teammate should step back helping you get through. In the guard-to-wing position the same techniques prevail. Go atop the screen if your opponent is in good shooting range. If she's not, go behind the screen; be the third player

27. Defense against screening

through. The player with the ball is number one. The screen is number two. And you are number three. Your teammate assigned to defend against the screener is number four. It is important that the number four player talks on defense, making the defensive player aware of exactly where the screen is.

If you are defending against a ball handler who sets a side screen, head up on the ball. Let your teammate know the ball is coming. When the ball is picked up, get back out of your teammate's way so that she can slide through behind the screen if the opponent receiving the basketball is out of scoring position. If the opponent is in scoring position, your teammate will slide over top, but it is important that you call out to her.

When defending against a stacked screen away from the ball, you must get off on the ball side of the screen quickly. Be ready to stop the offensive player cutting with the basketball. Once again talk among defensive players is very important. If a switch takes place, it should be called by the defensive player who is defending against the screener who then should switch to the player with the basketball.

Glossary

AIR BALL An ineffective shot that completely misses the back-board and rim.

ALLEY-OOP SHOT An acrobatic shot made by a player who goes high in the air and shoots the ball as she is falling to the ground.

ANTICIPATION A player's ability to sense ahead of time what an opposing player or team will do.

ASSIST A pass by one player to another that results in the second player scoring a basket.

BACKBOARD The surface that the basket is attached to (GLASS).

BACKCOURT The part of the court that contains the basket. There are actually two backcourts, as one team's backcourt is the other team's forecourt, depending on whether the team is playing offense or defense.

BACKCOURT FOUL Foul against an offensive player in her own backcourt.

BACKCOURT VIOLATION A professional rule that states a team must move the ball out of its backcourt within ten seconds after gaining possession. Failure to do this awards the ball to the other team.

BACK DOOR A situation where an offensive player goes behind the defense under her own basket to receive a pass.

BANK SHOT To use the backboard to make a shot via an angular carom of the ball into the basket, as opposed to shooting straight into the basket.

BASELINE The shorter boundary lines at either end of the court behind the basket.

BASKET An 18-inch-diameter metal ring from which a net is suspended and through which the ball must go for a field goal worth two points or a free throw worth one point (HOOP; HOLE).

BASKET-HANGER Also known as "hanger," a player who stays back under her basket while the other team is on offense; a quick pass to her from a teammate makes for a potentially easy basket. The problem with this strategy is that it leaves the basket-hanger's team shorthanded on defense.

BLOCKED SHOT A situation where a defensive player legally gets her hand on the ball held by an offensive player to hamper the shot.

BLOCKING Illegal movement of a defensive player into the path of an offensive player to interfere with free movement.

BOMB A shot at the basket taken from long range.

BONUS (FREE THROW) An extra foul shot awarded when a team uses up its allowance of fouls in a quarter of play. A fouled player in pro basketball gets two attempts for a one-shot foul, three attempts for a two-shot foul. High schools and colleges award the bonus for one-shot fouls; if the free throw is successful, there is another free throw awarded (PENALTY SHOT).

BONUS SITUATION After a team has used up its allowable fouls in a period, the bonus or penalty situation is applied.

BOUNCE PASS The passing of the ball on one bounce from one offensive player to another.

BOX OUT To position the body in front of another player in jockeying for rebounding position.

BUCKET A field goal (HOOP).

BUZZER SHOT One that scores a basket just as time elapses in a quarter.

CAGER Another name for a basketball player.

CENTER Pivotman, generally the tallest member of a team, who usually plays with her back to the basket on offense.

CENTER CIRCLE A four-foot circle located in the middle of the court and intersected by the division line. This marked-off area is used for the center jump at the start of each half.

CENTER JUMP A procedure used to begin play in each half that involves opposing centers jumping at the ball tossed up in the air at the center circle by the referee. Each center attempts to tap the ball to a teammate.

CHARGING A personal-foul violation committed when an offensive player runs into a defensive player who has established her position on the court. If the defensive player had moved into that position to interfere with the offensive player, the defensive player is guilty of blocking, and there is no charging violation.

CHARITY LINE The free-throw line (CHARITY STRIPE).

COLD Lacking the ability to score points (COLD STREAK).

CONTINUATION A flowing movement into a shot by a player so that if the player was fouled in making the shot, she can be awarded a free throw for being fouled in the act of shooting. If the shot is missed, a player can be awarded two free throws.

"D" Defense.

DEFENSIVE BOARD The backboard guarded by the defense.

DEFENSIVE REBOUND A rebound off the defensive board.

DIVISION LINE The midcourt line that divides the court in half (TIMELINE).

DOUBLE DRIBBLE A violation that gives the ball over to the other team; it is caused by a player starting her dribble, stopping, and then starting it again.

DOUBLE FIGURES The scoring of more than nine points in a game by a player.

DOUBLE-TEAM The guarding of one offensive player by two defensive players.

DOWNCOURT The area of the court opposite that where the action is taking place.

DOWNTOWN Shooting at the basket from an area that is a long distance from the backboard.

DRAW A FOUL To deliberately maneuver oneself so as to be fouled; to be fouled.

DRIBBLE To bounce and control the ball with one hand and walk or run with the ball at the same time.

DRIVE To dribble with speed toward the basket in a scoring attempt.

DUNK To leap high in the air and, with hand(s) above the rim, drop the ball through the basket for a score (STUFF).

FADEAWAY JUMP(ER) A jump shot at the basket in which the body of the player falls backward in getting the shot off.

FAST BREAK A quick breakaway downcourt to their basket by the team on offense.

FEED To pass the ball to another player, who then shoots it.

FIELD GOAL A basket scored from the floor and worth two points (HOOP).

FIELD-GOAL PERCENTAGE Ratio of shots taken to field goals scored.

FIVE-SECOND RULE An amateur rule that bans players from holding the ball in their forecourt for more than five seconds without making a move. Violation results in a jump ball at midcourt.

FOLLOW UP A situation where a player follows up a rebounded shot with another shot.

FORCE (FORCING) THE SHOT The act of a player shooting at the basket even though she is being defended effectively or does not have a good opportunity to make the shot.

FORECOURT The part of the court nearest the basket.

FORWARDS Two taller players who generally play in the corners on either side of their pivotman.

FOUL OUT To use up the allowed number of fouls and be forced to leave the game. In pro ball, six is the limit; in college, the limit is five.

FREE THROW An unguarded shot worth one point taken by a

player from the free-throw line for personal or technical fouls.

FREE-THROW AREA The part of the court that includes the free-throw line, the free-throw lane, and sometimes the free-throw circle.

FREE-THROW CIRCLE Located at either end of the court, these circles are bisected by the free-throw lines.

FREE-THROW LANE Bordered by the end line and the free-throw line, this lane is 19 feet long and 16 feet wide in pro basketball (THREE-SECOND LANE; THREE-SECOND AREA).

FREE-THROW LINE Parallel to the end line and 15 feet in front of the backboard, this 12-foot-long "charity stripe" is the line players must stand behind in taking free shots.

FREE-THROW PERCENTAGE The ratio of free throws made to free throws taken.

FRONT To attempt to deny the ball to a player by taking a defensive stance in front of her.

FRONTCOURT The area of the court closest to the basket for the team on offense.

FRONTCOURTMEN The two forwards and center.

FRONTLINE The three players who are frontcourtmen.

FULL-COURT PRESS Defensive guarding all over the court from the time the ball is inbounded by the team on offense.

GAME CLOCK The clock that indicates playing time used.

GARBAGE SHOOTER A player who specializes in taking and making easy shots close to the basket.

GET THE ROLL A phrase that describes a player's touch at the basket as the ball she has shot rolls on the rim and through the hoop.

GOAL Two points made on a shot from the field (BASKET).

GOALTENDING A violation caused by a player interfering with the ball after it begins its downward movement in an imaginary funnel over the rim.

GO BASELINE A phrase that describes a player on offense driving with the basketball along the baseline under the basket.

GUARDS Positions generally played by smaller players adept at ball handling and dribbling; they usually operate on the perimeter of the offensive and defensive zones.

GUNNER A player who shoots the ball whenever she can (CHUCKER).

HACK To hit an opponent's arm with the hand—a personal foul.

HAND CHECK The action of a defensive player who places her hand(s) on the body of the ball handler.

HANGER A defensive player who stays back under her offensive basket while her team is on defense and awaits the opportunity for her team to go on offense so that she is positioned for an easy shot.

HANG IN THE AIR A phrase that describes a player s ability to remain airborne for a brief moment—while taking a jump shot, for example.

HANG ON THE RIM The act of illegally placing the hands on the rim of the basket and hanging from that position.

HELD BALL A situation where two opposing players simultaneously have possession of the ball, causing a jump ball.

HELPING OUT To assist a teammate in defensive coverage.

HOLE The basket. Also, an area deep in the pivot area under the basket.

HOOK PASS A pass made by a player who raises her arm high over her head and arcs the ball to a teammate.

HOOK SHOT A type of shot in which a player positions the ball high over her head in the outstretched hand of her outstretched arm and arcs the ball at the basket.

HOOP A basket.

HOT HAND A phrase that describes a player or team on a streak of effective shooting.

INBOUNDS PLAY A situation where the ball is put into play after it has gone out of bounds or play has been stopped.

INTENTIONAL FOUL A deliberate foul generally committed late in a game to stop the clock, giving the opposition a chance at free throws in hopes that shots will be missed and the fouling team will gain ball possession.

JUMP BALL A situation where two opposing players leap up at a ball thrown by the referee and each attempts to tap it to her respective teammates; used at the start of the half and when disagreement as to who has the right to possession of the ball occurs.

JUMP PASS A type of pass where the player leaps in the air and passes the ball to a teammate.

JUMP SHOT A type of shot that involves a player jumping in the air and releasing the ball from a position over or behind her head.

KEYHOLE The free-throw lane and free-throw-circle area.

LAY-UP A close-in shot, usually after a drive to the basket.

LEAD PASS A pass ahead of a teammate, who runs for the ball.

LEAPER A player with top jumping ability.

LINE DRIVE A shot with no arc.

LOOSE-BALL FOUL In professional basketball, a personal foul by a player trying to get control of a loose ball. It is charged as a team foul, with the opposing team awarded possession of ball via a throw-in—except during a penalty situation, when two foul shots are given to the fouled player.

MAN-TO-MAN The guarding of one offensive player by one defensive player, as opposed to a zone.

MIDDLE The part of the court near the free-throw line.

MISMATCH A situation where a tall player by accident or missed assignment gets matched against a smaller player and gets a height advantage or vice versa.

OFFENSIVE FOUL A personal foul committed by a member of a team on offense.

OFFENSIVE REBOUND A rebound taken off the boards the offensive team is shooting at.

ONE-AND-ONE A bonus shot given in amateur ball if the first free shot is successful. In pro ball, the bonus shot is taken whether or not the first shot is made.

ONE-ON-ONE A man-to-man offensive and/or defensive action.

OPEN MAN An offensive player free to receive a pass with a good chance to take a good shot.

OPPORTUNITY SHOT A shot at the basket made available through luck or a defensive team's lapse.

OUTLET PASS A quick, long, downcourt pass generally made immediately after a rebound.

OUT OF BOUNDS A situation where a ball is no longer in play after touching or going over sidelines or baselines.

OUT-OF-BOUNDS PLAY A strategy used by a team in putting the ball back in play.

OUTREBOUND To rebound more effectively than another player or team.

PALMING Turning the ball over with a palm-twisting motion while dribbling—a violation that gives possession of the ball to the other team.

PASSING LANE An imaginary aisle between offensive players through which passes are made; the defense tries to protect against passes going through the passing lanes.

PENALTY SHOT A bonus free throw.

PENALTY SITUATION The condition of a team being in the bonus situation.

PENETRATION The ability by a player or team on offense to get in very close to the basket.

PERCENTAGE SHOT A shot at the basket that has a good chance to succeed.

PERSONAL FOUL Illegal physical contact by one player with another, such as charging, hacking, etc.

PICK A maneuver where an offensive player, by standing motionless, screens out a defensive player.

PICK-AND-ROLL A play where a pick is set and then the player moves off the pick and sprints toward the basket, anticipating a pass.

PIN To temporarily stop the ball on the backboard by pressing it there with a hand.

PIVOT To turn on one foot while keeping the pivot foot stationary.

PIVOTMAN A player who performs in the pivot or center position.

POINT GUARD A player who plays the guard position and directs her team's offense, generally from behind her team's offensive foul line.

POSITION The place on the court occupied by a player; good position is related to effective scoring, rebounding, and defense.

POST The pivot position; the high post is near the foul line for an offensive player; the low post is near the basket.

POWER FORWARD A strong rebounding and defensive forward.

PULL UP To drive to the basket with the ball, stop short, and, most times, shoot from this stopped position.

PUMP FAKE To feign shooting the ball up at the basket. A DOUBLE PUMP FAKE involves feigning a shot twice.

PURE SHOOTER A player who generally scores baskets cleanly and effortlessly.

PUSH OFF To illegally use the hands to push an opponent.

PUT THE BALL ON THE FLOOR To dribble the ball.

REBOUND To gain control of the ball as it comes off the backboard or rim after a missed shot.

REBOUNDER One who rebounds.

REFEREES The two or three officials who supervise all aspects of a basketball game. A TRAIL REFEREE is the one who follows the offensive flow of the game down the court. An ALTERNATE REFEREE is in attendance in pro basketball games to replace one of the three referees in case of an emergency or illness.

REVERSE DUNK The act of dunking the ball from an over-the-head or over-the-shoulder position opposite that to which the body is leaning.

REVERSE ENGLISH Reverse spin put on a shot.

RIM The basket's circular metal frame.

RIMMER A shot that rolls on the rim (RIMS THE RING).

ROLL To turn the body and move toward the basket.

ROUNDBALL Nickname for basketball (CAGE SPORT; HOOP GAME).

RUN-AND-GUN A high-powered running and shooting offense.

SAG To position the defense around a particular player or area by moving defensive players from other positions.

SAVE To keep a ball from going out of bounds.

SCOOP SHOT An underhand (running) shot taken close to basket.

SCREEN A maneuver where an offensive player gets stationary position in front of a teammate, thus acting as a human barrier or screen for her teammate to shoot over.

SET PLAY Prearranged offensive move(s).

SHORT A shot that does not touch the basket, but may touch the rim.

SHOT CLOCK A clock that indicates the time left for shooting; in the National Basketball Association, players must shoot within 24 seconds.

SIXTH MAN The first substitute usually used by a team—generally an excellent player.

SLAM DUNK A dunk that is forcefully jammed into a basket (STUFF).

SLOUGH OFF The act of a defender(s) leaving the player being guarded to aid in coverage of another opponent.

SPOT A favorite mark on the court from which a player shoots well.

STALL A maneuver where an offensive team late in a game slows down the action, and sometimes does not even shoot the ball, in an effort to control the game and the time (this tactic is not too feasible in professional basketball, with the 24-second clock).

STEAL A situation where a defensive player legally takes the ball away from an offensive player.

STEPS Walking, traveling.

STREAK SHOOTER One who makes a high percentage of her shots in spurts.

STUTTER STEP A quick, switching movement by a player from one foot to the other to fake out his opponent.

SWEEP THE BOARDS Rebound effectively.

SWING MAN A player capable of playing more than one position well.

SWISH A term that describes the scoring of a basket by getting the ball into the hoop without it touching the rim.

SWITCH To quickly exchange defensive assignments in the midst of play.

TAP IN To tip a ball into the basket off a rebound from the rim or backboard.

TEAM FOUL A foul charged to a team's quota for a period, which, when exceeded, allows the other team the bonus or penalty shot. The National Basketball Assocation allows four of these fouls per period, one in the final two minutes of a period, three in an overtime period.

TECHNICAL FOUL A misconduct penalty for violations such as abusive behavior that gives a free throw plus possession of the ball to the other team ("T"). In the NBA, the offending team regains possession of the ball.

TEN-SECOND RULE A professional regulation that requires an offensive team, after putting the ball in play, to bring it over the midcourt line within ten seconds, or else lose possession of the ball.

THREE-POINT PLAY A situation where a player who gets fouled while scoring a basket has the opportunity to score a third point on the play via a foul shot.

THREE-SECOND VIOLATION A regulation that bans an offensive player from remaining in the free-throw lane for more than three consecutive seconds.

THROW-IN To put a ball in play.

TIP-IN A quick follow-up shot made when a player pushes or taps the ball into the basket without first gaining control of the ball.

TOUCH A good feel for shooting the basketball.

TRAILER An offensive player who trails the offensive flow and comes late into a play.

TRAP A situation where defensive players double-team a player with the ball in an attempt to gain control of it (TRAP PRESS).

TRAVELING A rules violation where an offensive player walks with the ball by taking more steps without dribbling than allowed (STEPS; WALKING).

TWENTY-FOUR-SECOND RULE A professional and, in some cases, a college basketball regulation that requires the offensive team to shoot within twenty-four seconds after gaining possession of the ball; failure to do so as indicated on the twenty-four-second clock awards the ball to the other team.

WEAVE An arclike movement in a figure eight by offensive players aimed at freeing a player for an easy shot.

ZONE DEFENSE A condition that involves each defender guarding an area, not a player—illegal in professional basketball.

ZONE PRESS To press on defense in a particular area of the court.

Official Basketball Rules for Men and Women

As adopted by the International Amateur Basketball Federation, known as F.I.B.A. (Federation Internationale de Basketball Amateur)

Art. 1.   Definition

Basketball is played by two teams of five players each. The purpose of each team is to throw the ball into the opponents' basket and to prevent the other team from securing the ball or scoring. The ball may be passed, thrown, batted, rolled or dribbled in any direction, subject to the restrictions laid down in the following Rules.

Art. 2.   Court — Dimensions

The playing court shall be a rectangular hard surface free from obstructions and shall have dimensions of 26 m. in length by 14 m. in width, measured from the inside edge of the boundary lines.

The following variations in the dimensions are permitted: plus or minus 2 m. on the length and plus or minus 1 m. on the width, the variations being proportional to each other.

The height of the ceiling should be at least 7 m. The playing surface should be uniformly and adequately lighted. The light units should be placed where they will not hinder the vision of players.

Art. 3.   Boundary Lines

The playing court shall be marked by well-defined lines, which shall be at every point at least 1 m. from any obstruction. The lines of the long sides of the court shall be termed the **side lines,** those of the short sides, the **end lines.** The distance between these lines and the spectators should be at least 2 m.

When the margin of out-of-bounds free from obstruction is less than 1 m. a fine line should be drawn in the court 1 m. from the boundary line.

The lines mentioned in this article and in the following must be drawn so as to be perfectly visible and be 5 cm. in width.

Art. 4.   Centre Circle
The centre circle shall have a radius of 1.80 m. and it shall be marked in the centre of the court. The radius shall be measured to the outer edge of the circumference.

Art. 5.   Centre Line — Front Court, Back Court
A **Centre Line** shall be drawn, parallel to the end lines, from the mid-points of the side lines, and shall extend 15 cm. beyond each side line.

A **team's Front Court** is that part of the court between the end line behind the opponents' basket and the nearer edge of the centre line. The other part of the court, including the centre line, is the **team's Back Court.**

Art. 6.   Free Throw Lines
A **free throw line** shall be drawn parallel to each end line. It shall have its further edge 5.80 m. from the inner edge of the end line, and it shall be 3.60 m. long and its mid-point shall lie on the line joining the mid-points of the two end lines.

Art. 7.   Restricted Areas and Free Throw Lanes
The restricted areas shall be spaces marked in the court which are limited by the end lines, the free throw lines and by lines which originate at the end lines, their outer edges being 3 m. from the mid-points of the end lines, and terminate at the ends of the free throw lines.

The free throw lanes are the restricted areas extended in the playing court by semi-circles with a radius of 1.80 m. their centres at the mid-points of the free throw lines. Similar semi-circles shall be drawn with a broken line within the restricted areas.

Spaces along the free throw lanes, to be used by players during free throws, shall be marked as follows:
The first space shall be situated 1.80 m. from the inside edge of the end line, measured along the line at the side of the free throw lane, and shall be 85 cm. in width. The second space shall be adjacent to the first and shall also be 85 cm. in width. The lines used to mark these spaces shall be 10 cm. long and be per-

FULL SIZE REGULATION COURT

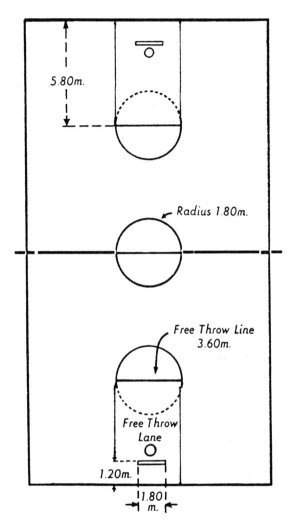

5.80m.

Radius 1.80m.

Free Throw Line
3.60m.

Free Throw
Lane

1.20m.

1.80
m.

All Lines 0.05m. Wide

pendicular to the side line of the free throw lane, and shall be drawn outside the space they are delimiting.

Art. 8. Backboards — Size, Material and Position

Each of the two backboards shall be made of hard wood, 3 cm. thick, or of a suitable transparent material (made in one piece and of the same degree of rigidity as those made of wood), and their dimensions shall be 1.80 m. horizontally and 1.20 m. vertically. The front surface shall be flat and unless it is transparent, it shall be white. This surface shall be marked as follows: a rectangle shall be drawn behind the ring and marked by a line 5 cm. in width. The rectangle shall have outside dimensions of 59 cm. horizontally and 45 cm. vertically. The top edge of its base line shall be level with the ring.

Borders of the backboards shall be marked with a line, 5 cm. in width. These lines shall be of a colour contrasting with the background. Normally, if the backboard is transparent it shall be marked, in white; in other cases in black. The edges of the backboards and the rectangles marked on them should be of the same colour.

The backboards shall be rigidly mounted in a position at each end of the court at right angles to the floor, parallel to the end lines, and with their lower edges 2.75 m. above the floor. Their centres shall lie in the perpendiculars erected at the points in the court 1.20 m. from the mid-points of the end lines. The up-rights supporting the backboards shall be at a distance of at least 40 cm. from the outer edge of end lines in the out-of-bounds area (it is strongly recommended that whenever possible, this distance should be 1.00 m.) and shall be of a **bright colour** in contrast with the background in such a manner that they will be clearly visible to the players. In addition, they shall be suitably padded to prevent injury.

Art. 9. Baskets

The baskets shall comprise the rings and the nets.

The rings shall be constructed from solid iron, 45 cm. in inside diameter, painted orange. The metal of the rings shall be 20 mm. in diameter, with the possible addition of small gauge loops on

REGULATION BASKET SUPPORT

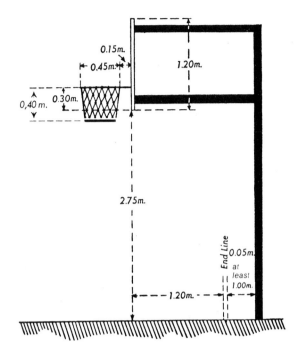

0.15m.

0.45m.

1.20m.

0.40 m.

0.30m.

2.75m.

End Line

0.05m.
at
least
1.00m.

1.20m.

REGULATION BACKBOARD MARKINGS

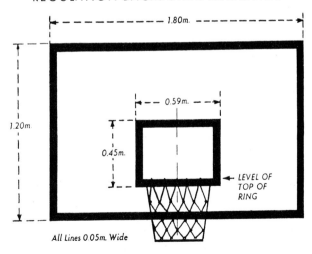

1.80m.

0.59m.

1.20m.

0.45m.

← LEVEL OF
TOP OF
RING

All Lines 0.05m. Wide

the under edge, or similar device for attaching the nets. They should be rigidly attached to the backboards and should lie in a horizontal plane 3.05 m. above the floor, equidistant from the two vertical edges of the backboard. The nearest point of the inside edge of the rings shall be 15 cm. from the faces of the backboards.

The nets shall be of white cord suspended from the rings and constructed in such a way so that they check the ball momentarily as it passes through the basket. They shall be 40 cm. in length.

Art. 10.   Ball – Material, Size and Weight

The ball shall be spherical; it shall be made of a rubber bladder covered with a case of leather, rubber or synthetic material; it shall be not less than 75 cm. nor more than 78 cm. in circumference; it shall weigh not less than 600 g. nor more than 650 g.; and it shall be inflated to an air pressure such that when it is dropped onto a solid wooden floor from a height of about 1.80 m., measured to the bottom of the ball, it will rebound to a height, measured to the top of the ball, of not less than about 1.20 m. nor more than about 1.40 m.

The home team shall provide a new ball or two good used balls satisfactory to the Referee. If used balls are provided, the Referee shall choose the one with which the game shall be played, and the visiting team shall have it as their practice ball. If a new ball is provided neither team shall use it in practice. If the ball provided by the home team is unsatisfactory to the Referee, he is hereby given authority to order the game to be played with the visiting team's ball if the latter is in a better condition.

Art. 11.   Technical Equipment

The following **technical equipment** shall be provided by the home team and shall be at the disposal of the Officials and their assistants:

(a) The **Game Watch** and the time-out watch; the Timekeeper shall be provided with at least two stop-watches, one of which shall be the game watch. It shall be placed on the table so that both the Timekeeper and the Scorer can see it.

(b) A suitable device, visible to players and spectators shall be provided for the administration of the **30-second Rule,** and shall be operated by the 30-second Operator.

(c) The official **Score Sheet** shall be the one approved by the International Amateur Basketball Federation, and it shall be filled in by the Scorer before and during the game as provided for in these Rules.

(d) There shall be suitable equipment for all signals provided for in these Rules, including a **Score Board** visible to players, spectators, and the Scorer's Table.

(e) **Markers numbered 1 to 5** shall be at the disposal of the Scorer. Every time a player commits a foul, the Scorer shall raise in a manner visible to both coaches the marker with the number corresponding to the the number of fouls committed by that player. The markers shall be white with black numbers from 1 to 4 and red for number 5.

(f) The Scorer shall be provided with **two team foul markers.** These shall be red flags constructed in such a way that when positioned on the Scorer's Table, they are easily visible to players, Coaches, and Officials. The moment the ball goes into play following the eighth player foul by a team, a flag shall be positioned on the Scorer's Table at the end nearer the bench of the team that has committed the eighth player foul.

RULE THREE   PLAYERS, SUBSTITUTES AND COACHES

Art. 12. Teams

Each team shall consist of ten players, one of whom shall be the Captain, and of a Coach who may be seconded by an Assistant Coach (see also art. 15). In tournaments where a team has to play more than five games the number of players in each team shall be increased to twelve.

Five players from each team shall be on the court during playing time (for exceptions see art. 33), and may be substituted within the provisions contained in these Rules.

Each player shall be numbered on the front and back of his shirt with plain numbers of solid colour contrasting with the colour of the shirt, and made of material not less than 2 cm. wide. The numbers on the back shall be at least 20 cm. high and those in the front at least 10 cm. high. Teams shall use numbers from 4 to 15.

Players on the same team shall not wear duplicate numbers.

Art. 13. Player Leaving Court
A Player may not leave the playing court during playing time without permission of an Official.

Art. 14. Captain — Duties and Powers
The Captain shall be the representative of his team and shall control its play (see also art. 90). The Captain may address an Official on matters of interpretation or to obtain essential information when necessary if it is done in a courteous manner. No other player may address an Official except as provided in art. 46.

Before leaving the playing court for any valid reason, the Captain shall inform the Referee regarding the player who will replace him during his absence.

Art. 15. Coaches
Before the game is scheduled to begin the Coach shall furnish the Scorer with names and numbers of players who are to play in the game, and with the name and number of the Captain of the team. If a player changes his number during the game he shall report the change to the Scorer and the Referee. Requests for charged time-outs shall be made by the Coach. When a Coach decides to request a substitution, he shall instruct the substitute to report to the Scorer. The player must be ready to play immediately (see art. 41 and 46, and Comments to art. 12, and Procedure before the Game).

If there is an Assistant Coach his name must be inscribed on the Score Sheet before the beginning of the game. He shall assume the responsibilities of the Coach if for any reason the Coach is unable to continue.

The team Captain may act as Coach. If he must leave the playing court for any valid reason, he may continue to act as Coach. However, if he must leave following a disqualifying foul, or if he is unable to act as Coach because of severe injury, his substitute as Captain shall also replace him as Coach.

RULE FOUR   OFFICIALS AND THEIR DUTIES

Art. 16.   Officials and their Assistants

The Officials shall be a Referee and an Umpire, who shall be assisted by a Timekeeper, a Scorer and a 30-second Operator.

It cannot be too strongly emphasized that the Referee and the Umpire of a given game should not be connected in any way with either of the organisations represented on the court, and that they should be thoroughly competent and impartial. The Officials have no authority to agree to changes in the Rules. Officials shall wear a uniform consisting of basketball or tennis shoes, long trousers, shirt or pullover, grey in colour.

Art. 17.   Duties and Powers of Referee

The Referee shall inspect and approve all equipment, including all the signals used by the Officials and their Assistants. He shall designate the official timepiece and recognise its operator, and shall also recognise the Scorer and the 30-second Operator. He shall not permit any player to wear objects which in his judgment are dangerous to other players.

The Referee shall toss the ball at centre to start the game. He shall decide whether a goal shall count if the Officials disagree. He shall have power to forfeit a game when conditions warrant. He shall decide matters upon which the Timekeeper and Scorer disagree. At the end of each half and of each extra period or at any time he feels necessary, he shall carefully examine the Score Sheet and approve the score, and confirm the time that remains to be played. His approval at the end of the game terminates the connection of the Officials with the game.

The Referee shall have power to make decisions on any point not specifically covered in the Rules.

Art. 18.   Duties of Officials — Referee and Umpire

The Officials shall conduct the game in accordance with the Rules. This includes: putting the ball in play, determining when the ball becomes dead and killing it with the whistle when necessary or blowing the whistle to stop action after the ball has become dead, administering penalties, ordering time-out, beckoning substitutes to come on the court, handing (not tossing) ball to a player when such player is to make a throw-in from out-of-bounds whenever this is provided for in these Rules (see art. 67 and 80) and silently counting seconds to administer provisions contained in art. 31, 58, 59, 60, 67 and 72.

Before the beginning of the game the Officials shall agree upon a division of the playing court, to be covered by each of them. After each foul or jump-ball decision, the Officials shall exchange their positions.

The Officials shall blow their whistles and simultaneously give the signal (no. 2 or no. 11) to stop the clock, followed by all the signals to make clear their decision. **The Officials shall not whistle** after a goal from the field or resulting from a free throw, but shall clearly indicate that a goal has been scored by using signal 23.

If verbal communication is necessary to make a decision clear, this must be done in English for all international games.

Art. 19.   Time and Place for Decisions

The Officials shall have powers to make decisions for infractions of the Rules committed either within or outside the boundary lines; these powers shall start when they arrive on the court, which shall be twenty minutes before the game is scheduled to begin and shall terminate with the expiration of playing time as approved by the Referee.

Penalties for fouls committed before the game or during intervals of play shall be administered as described in art. 74.

If during the period between the end of playing time and the signing of the Score Sheet there is any unsportsmanlike behaviour by players, Coaches, Assistant Coaches, or Team Followers, the Referee must record on the Score Sheet that an incident has occurred and ensure that a detailed report is submitted to the responsible authority which shall deal with the matter with appropriate severity.

Neither Official shall have authority to set aside or question decisions made by the other within the limits of his respective duties as outlined in these Rules.

If the Officials make approximately simultaneous decisions on the same play and the infractions involve different penalties, the more severe penalty shall be imposed. This does not prevent a double foul as defined in art. 83.

Art. 20. Calling of Fouls

When a foul is committed, the Official shall indicate the offender signalling his number to the Scorer with his fingers. If it is a personal foul involving a free throw penalty, the Official shall signal this clearly by indicating the free throw line; he shall also indicate the player who is to attempt the free throws. At this point, the Officials shall exchange their positions as provided for in art. 18. One of the Officials shall then administer the free throws or, if no free throw is involved, he shall hand the ball to the player who is to put it into play from the side line.

The Officials shall penalise unsportsmanlike conduct by any player, Coach, substitute or Team Follower. If there is a flagrant case of such conduct, the Officials shall penalise by removing any offending player from the game and banishing any offending substitute, Coach, attendant or Team Follower.

Art. 21. Duties of Scorer

The Scorer shall keep a chronological running summary of the points scored; he shall record the field goals made and the free throws made or missed. He shall record the personal and technical fouls called on each player and shall notify the Referee immediately when the fifth foul is called on any player. He shall record the time-outs charged to each team, and shall notify a Coach through an Official when he has taken a second time-out in each half. He shall also indicate the number of fouls committed by each player by using the numbered markers as provided in art. 11-e.

The Scorer shall keep a record of the names and numbers of players who are to start the game and of all substitutes who enter the game. When there is an infraction of the Rules pertaining to submission of line-up, substitutions or numbers of players, he shall notify the nearer Official as soon as possible when the infraction is discovered.

The sounding of the Scorer's signal does not stop the game. He should be careful to sound his signal only when the ball is dead and the game watch is stopped, and before the ball is again in play.

It is essential that the Scorer's signal be different from that of the Timekeeper and of the Officials.

Art. 22.   Duties of Timekeeper

The Timekeeper shall note when each half is to start and shall notify the Referee more than three minutes before this time so that he may notify the teams, or cause them to be notified, at least three minutes before the half is to start. He shall signal the Scorer two minutes before starting time. He shall keep record of playing time and time of stoppage as provided in these Rules.

For a charged time-out the Timekeeper shall start a time-out watch and shall direct the Scorer to signal the Referee when it is time to resume play.

The Timekeeper shall indicate with a gong, pistol or bell the expiration of playing time in each half, or extra period. This signal terminates actual playing time in each period. If the Timekeeper's signal fails to sound, or if it is not heard, the Timekeeper shall go on the court or use other means to notify the Referee immediately. If, in the meantime, a goal has been made or a foul has occurred, the Referee shall consult the Timekeeper and the Scorer. If they agree that the time was up before the ball was in the air on its way to the basket, or before the foul was committed, the Referee shall rule that the goal does not count or in case of a foul, that it shall be disregarded but if they disagree, the goal shall count or the foul be penalised unless the Referee has knowledge that would alter this ruling.

Art. 23. Duties of 30-second Operator

The 30-second Operator shall operate the 30-second device or watch (see art. 11-b) as provided in art. 62 in these Rules.

The signal of the 30-second Operator causes the ball to become a dead ball.

RULE FIVE   PLAYING REGULATIONS

Art. 24. Playing Time

The game shall consist of two halves of 20 minutes each, with an interval of 10 minutes between halves.

Note — If local conditions warrant it, the organisers may increase this interval to 15 minutes. This decision must be made known to all concerned before the beginning of the game. In tournaments lasting several days, the decision must be taken and made known to all concerned, at the latest, one day before the tournament is due to start.

Art. 25. Beginning of Game

The game shall be started by the Referee who shall toss the ball up for a centre jump between two opponents in the centre circle; the same procedure shall be followed at the beginning of the second half and, eventually, of each extra period.

The visiting team shall have choice of baskets in the first half; on neutral courts, teams shall toss for baskets. For the second half the teams shall change baskets.

The game cannot begin if one of the teams is not on the court with five players ready to play. If 15 minutes after the starting time the defaulting team is not present, the other team wins the game by forfeit.

Art. 26. Jump-Ball

A jump-ball takes place when the Official tosses the ball between two opposing players.

During a jump-ball the two jumpers shall stand with their feet inside that half of the circle which is nearer to their own baskets, with one foot near the centre of the line that is between them. The Official shall then toss the ball upward (vertically) in a plane at right angles to the side lines between the jumpers, to **a height greater than either of them can reach by jumping** and so that it will drop between them. The ball must be tapped by one or both of the jumpers **after** it reaches its highest point. If it touches the floor without being tapped by at least one of the jumpers, the Official shall put the ball in play again in the same place.

Neither jumper shall tap the ball before it reaches its highest point, nor leave their positions until the ball has been tapped. Either jumper may tap the ball twice only. After the second tap by a jumper he shall not touch the ball again until it has touched one of the eight non-jumpers, the floor, the basket or the backboard. Under this provision four taps are possible, two by each jumper. When a jump-ball takes place the eight non-jumpers shall remain outside the circle (cylinder) until the ball has been tapped. Team mates may not occupy adjacent positions around the circle if an opponent desires one of the positions.

During a jump-ball the Officials shall see that the other players are in such positions that they do not interfere with the jumpers.

Art. 27.   Violation during Jump-Ball

A player shall not violate provisions governing jump-ball. If, before the ball is tapped, a jumper leaves the jumping position or if a non-jumper enters the circle (cylinder), the Officials are authorised to give the violation arm signal but to withhold the whistle, to give opportunity for the opposing jumper to tap the ball into the basket, or to tap it in such a way that one of his team mates is first to touch the ball. If either of these occurs, the violation is disregarded. If both teams violate the jumping rule, or if the Official makes a bad toss, the toss shall be repeated.

Penalty: *see art. 65.*

Art. 28.   Goal — When Made and Its Value

A goal is made when a live ball enters the basket from above and remains in or passes through.

A goal from the field counts 2 points; **a goal from a free throw**

counts 1 point. A goal from the field counts for the team attacking the basket into which the ball is thrown.

If the ball accidentally enters the basket from below, it shall become dead and play shall be resumed by a jump-ball at the nearest free throw line.

If, however, a player deliberately causes the ball to enter the basket from below, it is a violation and play shall be resumed by an opponent throwing the ball in from the side line at the point nearest to where the violation occurred.

Art. 29. Interfere with the Ball in Offence

An offensive player may not touch the ball when it is on its downward flight and above the level of the ring **and is directly above the restricted area,** whether it is a shot for goal or a pass. This restriction applies only until the ball touches the ring.

An offensive player shall not touch his opponents' basket or backboard while the ball is on the ring during a shot for goal.

Penalty:

No point can be scored and the ball is awarded to opponents for a throw-in from out-of-bounds at a position on the side line nearest the point where the violation occurred (see art. 65).

Art. 30. Interfere with the Ball in Defence

A defensive player shall not touch the ball after it has started its downward flight during an opponent's shot for goal and while the ball is above the level of the ring. This restriction applies only until the ball touches the ring or until it is apparent it shall not touch it.

A defensive player shall not touch his own basket or backboard while the ball is on the ring during a shot for goal, or touch the ball or basket while the ball is within such basket.

Penalty:

The ball becomes dead when violation occurs. The thrower is awarded one point if during a free throw as in art. 73 and two points if during a shot for goal. Ball is awarded out-of-bounds from behind the end line as though the throw had been successful and there had been no violation.

161

Art. 31. Ball in Play after Goal

After a goal from the field, any opponent of the team credited with the score shall put the ball in play from any point out-of-bounds at the end of the court where the goal was made. He may throw it from any point behind the end line, or he may pass it to a team mate behind the end line. Not more than 5 seconds may be consumed in getting the ball in play, the count starting the instant the ball is at the disposal of the first player out-of-bounds.

The Official should not handle the ball unless by so doing he can get the ball in play more quickly. Opponents of the player who is to put the ball in play shall not touch the ball. Allowance may be made for touching the ball accidentally or instinctively but if a player delays the game by interfering with the ball, it is a technical foul.

After the last free throw, the ball shall be thrown in from out-of-bounds:

(a) by any opponent of the free thrower from behind the end line if the throw is successful or

(b) by any player of the free thrower's team from out-of-bounds at mid-court if the free throw is for a technical foul by Coach, Assistant Coach, substitute, or Team Follower, whether or not the throw is successful (see art. 78—penalty).

Art. 32. Decision of Game

A game shall be decided by the scoring of the greater number of points in the playing time.

Art. 33. Game to be Forfeited

Captains shall be notified three minutes before the termination of the interval between halves. If either team is not on the floor ready to play within one minute after the Referee calls play, either at the beginning of the second half or after time has been taken out for any reason, the ball shall be put in play in the same manner as if both teams were on the floor ready to play, and the absent team shall forfeit the game.

A team shall forfeit the game if it refuses to play after being instructed to do so by the Referee.

When during a game the number of players of a team on the court shall be less than two, the game shall end, and that team shall lose the game by forfeit.

If the team to which the game is forfeited is ahead, the score at the time of forfeiture shall stand. If this team is not ahead, the score shall be recorded as 2 to 0 in its favour.

Art. 34. Tie Score and Extra Periods

If the score is a tie at the expiration of the second half, play shall be continued for an **extra period** of 5 minutes or as many such periods of 5 minutes as may be necessary to break the tie. Before the first extra period the teams shall toss for baskets and shall change baskets at the beginning of each additional extra period. An interval of 2 minutes shall be allowed before each extra period. At the beginning of each extra period, the ball shall be put in play at the centre.

Art. 35. When Game is Terminated

The game shall terminate at the sounding of the Timekeeper's signal indicating the end of playing time.

When a foul is committed simultaneously with or just previous to the Timekeeper's signal ending a half or an extra period, time shall be allowed for the free throw or throws, if any are involved in the penalty.

When a shot (see art. 57) is taken near the end of playing time the goal, if made, shall count if the ball was in the air before time expired. All provisions contained in art. 29 and 30 shall apply until the ball touches the ring. If the ball strikes the ring, rebounds and then enters the basket, the goal shall count. If, after the ball has touched the ring, a player of either team touches the ball, it is a violation. If a defensive player commits such a violation, two points shall be awarded. If an offensive player commits such a violation, the ball becomes dead and the goal, if scored, shall not count. These provisions apply until it is apparent the shot will not be successful.

Art. 36.   Game Watch Operations

The game watch shall be started when the ball after having reached its highest point on a toss at the beginning of a half or extra period, is tapped by the first player.

The game watch shall be stopped at the expiration of time for each period of play.

Art. 37.   Ball goes into play

The ball goes into play (is in play) when

- (a) the Official enters the circle to administer a jump-ball, or
- (b) the Official enters the free throw lane to administer a free throw (see art. 72), or
- (c) when in an out-of-bounds situation the ball is at the disposal of the player who is at the point of the throw-in.

Art. 38.   Ball Becomes Alive

The ball becomes alive when

- (a) after having reached its highest point in a jump-ball it is tapped by the first player, or
- (b) when the Official places it at the disposal of a free thrower (see art. 72), or
- (c) when on a throw-in from out-of-bounds it touches a player in the court.

Art. 39.   Dead Ball

The ball becomes dead when

- (a) any goal is made (see art. 28),
- (b) any violation occurs,
- (c) a foul occurs while the ball is alive or in play,
- (d) held ball occurs or the ball lodges on the basket support,
- (e) it is apparent that the ball will not go into the basket; on a free throw for a technical foul by Coach or substitute, or a free throw which is to be followed by another throw,
- (f) Official's whistle is blown while the ball is alive or in play,

(g) the 30-second Operator's signal is sounded while the ball is alive,

(h) time expires for a half or extra period.

Exceptions:

The ball does not become dead at the time of the listed act and goal, if made, counts, if

(1) ball is in flight on a free throw or a shot for goal when (c), (f), (g) or (h) occurs, or

(2) an opponent fouls while the ball is still in control of a player who is shooting for goal and who finished his shot with a continuous motion which started before the foul occurred, or

(3) penalty for a jump-ball violation is ignored.

Art. 40. Time Out

Time Out occurs and the game watch shall be stopped when an Official signals:

(a) a violation,

(b) a foul,

(c) a held ball,

(d) unusual delay in getting a dead ball into play,

(e) suspension of play for an injury, or for removal of a player, such removal being ordered by an Official,

(f) suspension of play for any reason, ordered by the Officials,

(g) when the 30-second signal is sounded, or

(h) when a basket is scored against the team of a Coach who has requested a charged time-out.

Art. 41. Charged Time-out

A Coach has the right to request a charged time-out. He shall do so by going in person to the Scorer and asking clearly for a "time-out," making the proper conventional sign with his hands.

Electrical devices enabling Coaches, if they so wish, to request a time-out without leaving their places may be used. Such devices may not, under any circumstances, be used to request a player substitution.

The Scorer shall indicate to the Officials that a request for charged time-out has been made by sounding his signal as soon as the ball is dead and the game watch is stopped **but before the ball is again in play** (see art. 37).

A Coach may also be granted a charged time-out, if, after a request from him for a time-out, a field goal is scored by his opponents. In this case the Timekeeper shall immediately stop the game watch. The Scorer shall then sound his signal and indicate to the Officials that a charged time-out has been requested.

A charged time-out shall not be granted from the moment the ball is in play for the first or only free throw until the ball becomes dead after being alive again after the free throw or throws.

A time-out shall be charged to a team for each minute consumed under these provisions. If the team responsible for the time-out is ready to play before the end of the charged time-out, the Referee is hereby given authority to start the game immediately.

Exceptions: No time-out is charged if an injured player is ready to play immediately or is substituted as soon as possible or if a disqualified player, or a player who has committed his fifth foul is replaced within one minute, or if an Official permits a delay.

Art. 42.   Legal Charged Time-out

Two charged time-outs may be granted to each team during each half of playing time, and one charged time-out for each extra period.

Unused time-outs may not be carried over to the next half or extra period.

Art. 43.   Time-out in Case of Injury

The Officials may order time-out in case of injury to players or for any other reason, although not for trifles. If the ball is alive when an injury occurs, the Officials shall withhold their whistles until the play has been completed, that is, the team in possession of the ball has thrown for goal, lost possession of the ball, has withheld the ball from play, or the ball has become a dead ball.

When necessary to protect an injured player, the Officials may suspend play immediately.

If the injured player cannot continue to play immediately, he must be substituted within one minute or as soon as possible, should the injury prevent an earlier substitution. If free throws have been awarded to the injured player, they must be attempted by his substitute. If this occurs, the provisions contained in the last paragraph of art. 46, Exception, shall not apply. If an injured player is not substituted as set out in this article, his team shall be charged with a time-out, except in the case of a team having to continue with fewer than five players. If his team has no charged time-outs left, a technical foul shall be charged against the Coach.

Art. 44.   Time in

After time has been out, the game watch shall be started:

(a) if play is resumed by a jump-ball, when the ball after reaching its highest point is tapped by the first player,

(b) if a free throw is not successful and the ball is to continue in play, when the ball touches a player on the court,

(c) if play is resumed by throw-in from out-of-bounds, when the ball touches a player on the court.

Art. 45.   How Play is Resumed

After time-out or after the ball has become dead for any other reason, ball is put in play as follows:

(a) **if a team had control** of the ball, any player of that team shall throw it in from the point out-of-bounds on the side lines nearest the point where the ball became dead,

(b) **if neither team had control,** ball is put in play by a jump-ball at the circle nearest where the ball became dead,

(c) **after a foul,** ball is put in play by placing it at the disposal of the offended team (out-of-bounds on the side line) or the free thrower or by a jump-ball at the nearest circle (see also art. 80—Penalty, 2-i),

(d) **after a held ball,** or the ending of a half-period, or a field goal or an out-of-bounds, or the ending of a free throw, or a violation, ball is put in play as prescribed in the relevant Rule.

RULE SEVEN   PLAYERS' REGULATIONS

Art. 46.   Substitutions

A substitute before going upon the court shall report to the Scorer and must be ready to play immediately.

The Scorer shall sound his signal immediately if the ball is dead and the game watch stopped, or as soon as the ball becomes dead and the game watch is stopped, but before the ball is again in play (see art. 37), as the consequence of one of the following situations:

(a) a held ball has been called,
(b) a foul has been called,
(c) a charged time-out has been granted,
(d) game has been stopped to attend an injured player, or for any other reason, ordered by the Officials.

Following a violation, only the team who has possession of the ball for the throw-in from out-of-bounds may effect a substitution, if such a situation occurs, the opponents may also effect a substitution.

The substitute shall remain outside the boundary line until an Official beckons him to enter whereupon he shall report immediately to the nearer Official indicating the number of the player he replaces. When a substitute enters at the beginning of the second half, he is not required to report to an Official, but he must report to the Scorer.

Substitutions shall not take more than 20 seconds, regardless of the number of substitutions effected by one team. If more time is taken, it shall count as a time-out and shall be charged against the offending team.

A player involved in a jump-ball may not be substituted by another player.

A substitution is not permitted from the moment the ball is in play for the first or only free throw until the ball becomes dead after being alive again after the free throw or throws.

Exception: After a successful last free throw only the player who was attempting the free throw may be substituted, providing such substitution was requested before the ball went into play for the first or only free throw, in which case the opponents may be granted one substitution provided the request is made before the ball goes into play for the last free throw.

Art. 47.   Location of Player and Official

The location of a player is determined by where he is touching the floor. When he is in the air from a leap, he retains the same status as when he last touched the floor as far as the boundary lines, the centre line, the free throw line or the lines delimiting the free throw lanes are concerned (except as provided in art. 68-b).

The location of an Official is determined in the same manner as that of a player. When the ball touches an Official it is the same as touching the floor at the Official's location.

Art. 48.   How Ball is Played

In Basketball the ball is played with the hands. *Kicking or striking it with the fist is a violation. For penalty see art. 65.*

Kicking the ball is a violation only when it is a positive act; accidentally striking the ball with the foot or leg is not a violation.

Art. 49.   Control of the Ball

A player is in control when he is holding or dribbling a live ball or in an out-of-bounds situation when the ball is at his disposal for a throw-in (see art. 37-c).

A team is in control when a player of that team is in control and also when the ball is being passed between team mates.

Team control continues until an opponent secures control, or the ball becomes dead, or on a shot for goal when the ball is no longer in contact with the hand of the shooter.

Art. 50. Player Out-of-Bounds — Ball Out-of-Bounds

A player is out-of-bounds when he touches the floor on or outside the boundary lines.

The ball is out-of-bounds when it touches a player who is out-of-bounds or any other person, the floor or any object on or outside a boundary line, or the supports or back of the backboards.

Art. 51. How Ball Goes Out-of-Bounds

If the ball is out-of-bounds because of touching something other than a player, it is caused to go out by the last player to touch it before it goes out. If it is out-of-bounds because of touching a player (on or outside boundary), such a player causes it to go out. If a player deliberately throws or taps the ball onto an opponent, thus causing it to go out-of-bounds, the ball shall be awarded to the opponents, even though it was last touched by that team (see art. 62).

An Official shall clearly indicate the team which shall put the ball in play from out-of-bounds. Out-of-bounds decisions should be clearly signalled by the Officials. If there is doubt about players understanding the decision, the Official should secure the ball and delay the throw-in until the decision has been made clear (see also art. 56).

To cause the ball to go out-of-bounds is a violation. For penalty see art. 65.

Officials should declare jump-ball when they are in doubt as to which team caused the ball to go out-of-bounds.

Art. 52. Pivot

A pivot takes place when a player who is holding the ball steps once or more than once in any direction with the same foot, the other foot called the pivot foot, being kept at its point of contact with the floor.

Art. 53. Dribbling

A dribble is made when a player, having gained control of the ball, gives impetus to it by throwing, tapping or rolling it and touches it again before it touches another player. In a dribble the ball must come in contact with the floor. After giving impetus to the ball as described in the foregoing, the player completes his dribble the instant he touches the ball simultaneously with both hands, or permits the ball to come to rest in one or both hands. There is no limit to the number of steps a player may take when the ball is not in contact with his hand, he may take as many steps as he wishes between bounces of a dribble.

A player is entitled to a dribble each time he gains control of the ball. After completing a dribble he may not dribble again until he has lost and then regained control of the ball. He loses control the moment the ball leaves his hand(s) on a shot or a pass, or has been batted or taken out of his possession by an opponent.

A player who throws the ball against a backboard and touches it before it touches another player commits a second dribble violation unless in the opinion of the official it was a shot.

Exception: The following are not dribbles: successive tries for goal, fumbles, attempts to gain control of the ball by tapping it from the vicinity of other players striving for it, batting it from the control of another player, blocking a pass and recovering the ball, or tossing the ball from hand(s) to hand(s) and permitting it to come to rest before touching the floor, provided he does not commit a progressing with the ball violation.

To make a second dribble is a violation. For penalty, see art. 65.

Art. 54. Progressing with the Ball

A player may progress with the ball in any direction within the following limits:

ITEM I — A player who receives the ball while standing still may pivot, using either foot as the pivot foot.

ITEM II — A player who receives the ball while he is progressing or upon completion of a dribble may use a **two-count rhythm** in coming to a **stop** or in **getting rid of the ball.**

The first count occurs:

(a) as he receives the ball if either foot is touching the floor at the time he receives it, or

(b) as either foot touches the floor or as both feet touch the floor simultaneously after he receives the ball if both feet are off the floor when he receives it.

The second count occurs when, after the count of one, either foot touches the floor or both feet touch the floor simultaneously.

When a player **comes to a legal stop,** if one foot is in advance of the other he may pivot but the rear foot only may be used as the pivot foot. However, if neither foot is in advance of the other, he may use either foot as the pivot foot.

ITEM III — A player who receives the ball while standing still or who comes to a legal stop while holding the ball,

  (a) **may lift the pivot foot or jump** when he throws for goal or passes, but the ball must leave his hands before one or both feet again touch the floor

  (b) **may not lift the pivot foot,** in starting a dribble, before the ball leaves his hands.

To progress with the ball in excess *of these limits is a violation. For penalty see art. 65.*

Art. 55. Held Ball

A held ball shall be declared when two or more players of opposing teams have one or both hands firmly on the ball.

Officials should not declare held ball too quickly, thereby interrupting the continuity of the game, and unjustly taking the ball from the player who gained or is about to gain possession. Under the first clause of this article, held ball should not be called until at least one player from each team has one or both hands firmly on the ball so that neither player could gain possession without undue roughness.

A held ball decision is not warranted merely on the grounds that the defensive player gets his hands on the ball. Usually such a decision is unfair to the player who has firm possession of the ball.

If a player is lying or sitting on the floor while in possession of the ball, he should have opportunity to play it, but held ball should be called if there is danger of injury.

When held ball is called, the ball shall be tossed up between the two contending players at the nearest circle. In case of doubt as to which is the nearest circle, the ball shall be tossed up at the centre.

If there are more than two players involved, the ball shall be tossed up between two contending players of approximately the same height.

Art. 56.   Jump-Ball in Special Situations

If the ball goes out-of-bounds and was last touched simultaneously by two opponents, or if the Official is in doubt as to who last touched the ball, or if the Officials disagree, play shall be resumed by a jump-ball between the two involved players at the nearest circle.

Whenever the ball lodges on the basket supports, it shall be put in play by a jump-ball between any two opponents on the nearer free throw line, except when such a situation arises during a free throw following a technical foul by Coach or substitute (see art. 78), in which case the ball shall be put in play in the prescribed manner.

Art. 57.   Player in the Act of Shooting

A player is in the act of shooting when in the judgement of an Official, he starts an attempt to score by throwing, dunking, or tapping the ball and it continues until the ball has left the player's hand(s).

Exception: Players who tap the ball towards the basket directly from a jump-ball are not considered to be in the act of shooting. (For definition of throw, dunk and tap, see Comments to art. 57).

Art. 58.   Three-second Rule

A player shall not remain for more than three seconds in that part of the opponents' restricted area, between the end line and the farther edge of the free throw line, while the ball is in control of his team. The 3-second restriction is in force in all out-of-bounds situations, and the count shall start at the moment the player throwing-in is out-of-bounds and has control of the ball.

The lines bounding the restricted area are part of it and a player touching one of these lines is in the area. The 3-second restriction does not apply while the ball is in the air on a try for a goal, or while it is rebounding from the backboard, or is dead, because the ball is not in control of either team at such times. Allowance may be made for a player who, having been in the restricted area for less than 3 seconds, dribbles in to throw for goal.

An infraction of this rule is a violation. For penalty, see art. 65.

Art. 59.   Five-second Rule

Held ball shall be called when a closely guarded player who is holding the ball does not pass, shoot, roll or dribble the ball within five seconds.

Art. 60.   Ten-second Rule

When a team gains control of a live ball in its back court, it must, within ten seconds cause the ball to go into its front court.

The ball goes into a team's front court when it touches the court beyond the centre line or touches a player of that team who has part of his body in contact with the court beyond the centre line.

An infraction of this Rule is a violation. For penalty, see art. 65.

Art. 61.   Ball Returned to Back Court

A player in his front court may not cause the ball to go into his back court. It is caused to go into the back court by the last player to touch it before it goes into the back court. This restriction applies to all situations occurring in a team's front court, including a throw-in from out-of-bounds, rebounds and interceptions. It does not apply, however, to jump-ball situations at the centre circle or to the situation described in art. 78 (Penalty) and in art. 90.

A player in his front court who gains control of the ball directly from a jump-ball at the centre circle, may pass the ball into his back count.

The ball goes into a team's back court when it touches a player of that team who has part of his body in contact with the centre line or with the court beyond the centre line, or is touched by a player of that team after it has touched the back court.

Penalty:

The ball is awarded to an opponent for a throw-in from the mid-point of a side line and he shall be entitled to pass the ball to a player at any point on the playing court.

Art. 62.   Thirty-second Rule

When a team gains control of a live ball on the court a shot for goal must be made within 30 seconds.

Failure to do so is a violation of this rule. For penalty see art. 65.

If the ball goes out-of-bounds during the 30-second period, and the ball is awarded to the same team, a new 30-second period shall begin. The mere touching of the ball by an opponent does not start a new 30-second period if the same team remains in control of the ball.

If a player deliberately throws or bats the ball into an opponent, causing it to go out-of-bounds, the ball shall be awarded to the opponents, even though it was last touched by that team. This provision is made to prevent a team from illegally obtaining a new 30-second period.

All regulations concerning the end of playing time shall apply to violations of the 30-second Rule.

RULE EIGHT   INFRACTIONS AND PENALTIES

Art. 63.   Violations and Fouls

A violation is an infraction of the Rules, the penalty for which is the loss of the ball.

When an infraction involves a personal contact with an opponent or unsportsmanlike conduct, **the violation becomes a foul,** which will be inscribed against the offender and the consequence of which is a penalty administered according to the provisions contained in the relevant article of these Rules.

Art. 64.   Ball in Play after Violation or Foul

After the ball has become dead following an infraction of the Rules, the ball is put in play:

(a) by a throw-in from out-of-bounds, or
(b) by a jump-ball at one of the circles, or
(c) by one or more free throws.

Art. 65. Procedure when a Violation is Called

When a violation is called the ball becomes dead. The ball is awarded to a nearby opponent for a throw-in from the side line nearest the spot where the violation occurred. If the ball goes into a basket during the dead ball which follows such a violation, no point can be scored.

Art. 66. Procedure when Foul is Called

When a player foul is called the Official shall signal to the Scorer the number of the offender. The player thus indicated shall turn to face the Scorer's Table, and shall immediately raise his hand above his head. For failure to do so, after having been warned once by the Official, a technical foul may be called against the offending player.

If the foul was committed on a player who was not in the act of shooting, the Official shall hand the ball to him or to one of his team mates for a throw-in from the side line at a spot nearest the place of the foul (see also art. 92).

If the foul was committed on a player in the act of shooting,

(a) if the goal is made it shall count, and, in addition, one free throw shall be awarded,

(b) if the goal is missed, the Official shall take the ball to the free throw line and shall put it at the disposal of the free thrower unless play is to be resumed by a jump-ball, as in the case of a double foul.

Art. 67. How Ball is Put in Play from Out-of-Bounds

The player who is to throw the ball in from out-of-bounds, shall stand out-of-bounds at the side line at a spot nearest the point where the ball left the court, or the violation or foul was committed. Within 5 seconds from the time the ball is at his disposal, he shall throw, bounce or roll the ball to another player within the court. While the ball is being passed into the court no other player shall have any part of his body over the boundary line. When the margin of out-of-bounds territory free from obstruction is less than 1 m., no player of either team shall be within 1 m. of the player who is putting the ball in play.

Whenever the ball is awarded to a team out-of-bounds at the side line in its front court, an Official must hand the ball to the player who is to put it in play. The purpose of this is to make the decision clear, and not to delay the game until the defensive team gets "set."

Whenever the ball is awarded to a team out-of-bounds at the side line in its back court, the Official, if there is confusion as to the decision, shall hand the ball to the thrower-in at the side line closest to the violation.

Art. 68. Violation on Out-of-Bounds Play

A player shall not violate provisions governing a throw-in from out-of-bounds. These provisions:

(a) forbid a player who has been awarded the ball for a throw-in to touch it in the court before it has touched another player, or to step on the line or the court whilst releasing the ball, or to consume more than 5 seconds before releasing the ball,

(b) forbid any other player to have any part of his body over the boundary line before the ball has been thrown across the line or to put the ball in play after the Official has awarded it to the other team.

Penalty:
(1) If infraction is of (a), see art. 65,
(2) if infraction is of (b), see art. 77, penalty.

Art. 69. How Ball is Put in Play by a Jump-Ball

Whenever the ball must be put in play by a jump-ball, this will be done in the manner described in art. 26.

Art. 70. Free Throws

A free throw is a privilege given a player to score one point by an unhindered throw for goal from a position directly behind the free throw line (see art. 72).

Art. 71.   Player to Attempt Free Throw

When a personal foul is called, and a free throw penalty is awarded, the player upon whom the foul was committed shall be designated by the Official to attempt the free throws. If any other player attempts the throw, it shall not count if made, and whether made or missed, the ball shall be awarded to an opponent out-of-bounds at the side line opposite the free throw line.

Should a player, by mistake, execute a free throw into his own basket, the try shall be annulled, whether successful or not, and a new try shall be granted at the other basket.

If the designated player must leave the game because of injury, his substitute must attempt the free throws. If the player who has been fouled is to leave the game because of a substitution, he shall attempt the free throws before leaving (see art. 46). When there is no substitute available the free throws may be attempted by the Captain or by any player designated by him.

When a technical foul is called, the free throw or throws may be attempted by any player of the opposing team.

Art. 72.   How a Free Throw is Attempted

The throw for goal shall be made within 5 seconds after ball has been placed at the disposal of the free thrower at the free throw line. This shall apply to each free throw.

The player who is to attempt the free throws shall take a position immediately behind the free throw line, and shall be free to use any system in throwing the ball but he shall not touch the free throw line or the court beyond the line until the ball touches the ring.

Players may not attempt to disconcert the thrower by their action. Neither Official shall stand in the free throw area (restricted area) or behind the backboard.

When a player is attempting a free throw, the other players shall be entitled to take the following positions:

(a) two players from the opposing team, the two places nearer the basket,

(b) the other players shall take alternate positions,

(c) all other players may take any other position, provided that:

(i) they neither disturb nor are in the way of the free thrower and of the Officials,

(ii) they do not move from their positions before the ball has touched the ring,

(iii) they do not occupy the places along the free throw lane next to the end line.

On free throws following technical fouls by Coach, Assistant Coach, substitutes, or Team Followers, players shall not line up along the free throw lane (see art. 78—penalty.)

Art. 73. Violation of Free Throw Provisions

After the ball has been placed at the disposal of the free thrower:

(a) he shall throw within 5 seconds and in such a way that the ball enters the basket or touches the ring before it is touched by a player,

(b) neither he nor any other player shall touch the ball or basket while the ball is on its way to the basket or is on or within the basket,

(c) he shall not touch the floor on or across the free throw line and no other player of either team shall touch the free throw lane or disconcert the thrower. This restriction applies until the ball touches the ring or until it is apparent it will not touch it.

Penalty:

(1) *If the violation is by the free thrower only, no point can be scored. Ball becomes dead when violation occurs. Ball is awarded out-of-bounds on the side line, to the free thrower's team opposite centre circle after a technical foul by Coach, Assistant Coach, substitute, or Team Followers, and to the free thrower's opponents opposite the free throw line after a player foul.*

(2) *If violation of (b) is by a team mate of the free thrower, no point can be scored and violation shall be penalised as above. If violation of (b) is by both teams no point can be scored and play shall be resumed by a jump-ball on the free throw line.*

If violation of (b) is by the free thrower's opponents only violation is penalised as indicated in art. 30 (Penalty).

(3) If violation of (c) is by a team mate of the free thrower and the free throw is successful, the goal shall count and violation be disregarded. If the free throw is not successful, violation shall be penalised as above. However, if the ball misses the ring and goes out-of-bounds or falls within bounds, it shall be put in play by the opponents from the side line opposite the free throw line.

(4) If the violation of (c) is by the free thrower's opponents only, and the throw is successful, the goal shall count and violation disregarded; if it is not successful, a substitute throw shall be attempted by the same thrower.

(5) If there is a violation of (c) by both teams and the free throw is successful, the goal shall count and violation be disregarded. If the free throw is not successful play shall be resumed by a jump-ball on the free throw line.

If there is a multiple throw, the out-of-bounds and jump-ball provisions apply only to violation during the last free throw.

Art. 74. Technical Foul before the Game or during an Interval of Play

If a technical foul is called before the game, during the half-time, or during an interval before an extra period, the penalty shall be two free throws and play shall be started or resumed by a jump-ball at the centre after the throws have been attempted.

Art. 75. Ball in Play if Free Throw is Missed

If the goal is missed, the ball shall continue in play after the last free throw following a player foul. If the ball misses the ring, it is a violation (see art. 73, penalty (1)) and the ball shall be put in play from the side line at the point opposite the free throw line by the opposing team.

In case of a free throw following a tecbnical foul by Coach, Assistant Coach, substitute, or Team Followers, see art. 31-b.

RULE NINE	RULES OF CONDUCT

A. Relationships

Art. 76. Definition

The proper conduct of the Game demands the full and loyal co-operation of members of both teams, including Coaches and substitutes, with the Officials and their assistants.

Both teams are entitled to do their best to secure victory, but this must be done in a spirit of sportsmanship and fairplay.

An infringement of this co-operation or of this spirit, when deliberate or repeated, should be considered as a **Technical Foul** and penalised as provided in the following articles of these Rules.

Art. 77. Technical Foul by Player

A player shall not disregard admonitions by Officials or use unsportsmanlike tactics, such as:

(a) disrespectfully addressing or contacting an Official,

(b) using language or gestures likely to give offence,

(c) baiting an opponent or obstructing his vision by waving hands near his eyes,

(d) delaying the game by preventing ball from being promptly put in play,

(e) not raising his hand properly when a foul is called on him (see art. 66),

(f) changing his playing number without reporting to Scorer and to Referee,

(g) enter the court as a substitute without reporting to Scorer, or without reporting promptly to an Official (unless between halves), or during a time-out after having withdrawn during the same time-out,

(h) grasping the ring; a player who violates this provision must be promptly penalised by a technical foul awarded against him.

181

Technical infractions which are obviously unintentional and have no effect on the game, or are of an administrative character, are not considered technical fouls unless there is repetition of the same infraction after a warning by an Official to the offending player and to his Captain.

Technical infractions which are deliberate or are unsportsmanlike or give the offender an unfair advantage, should be penalised promptly with a technical foul.

Penalty:

A foul shall be charged and recorded for each offence and two free throws awarded to the opponents for each foul and the Captain shall designate the thrower. For flagrant or persistent infraction of this article, a player shall be disqualified and removed from the game.

If discovery of such a foul is after ball is in play following the foul, penalty should be administered as if the foul had occurred at the time of discovery. Whatever occurred in the interval between the foul and its discovery shall be valid.

Art. 78.   Technical Foul by Coaches, Substitutes, or Team Followers

The Coach, Assistant Coach, substitutes, or Team Followers shall not enter the court unless by permission of an Official to attend an injured player, nor leave their place to follow the action on the court from the boundary lines, nor disrespectfully address Officials (including Scorer, Timekeeper and 30-second Operator), or opponents.

A Coach may address players of his team during a charged time-out provided he does not enter the playing court and players do not cross the boundary line (unless permission is first obtained from an Official). Substitutes may also listen in provided they do not enter the playing court.

The distinction between unintentional and deliberate infractions (see art. 77) applies also to infractions committed by Coaches, Assistant Coaches, substitutes, and Team Followers.

Penalty:

A foul shall be charged and inscribed against the Coach and one free throw awarded for each offence, and the opposing Captain shall designate the thrower. During the free throw players shall not line up along the free throw lanes. After the throw, the ball shall be put in play by any player of the free thrower's team from out-of-bounds at mid-court on the side line, whether or not the throw is successful.

Technical fouls may be called during intervals of play (see art. 74). If called against the Coach, the Assistant Coach or Team Follower, the penalty shall be two free throws and a foul inscribed against the coach of that team. If called against a player or a substitute, a technical foul shall be charged against him and two free throws awarded to the opponents.

For a flagrant infraction of this article, or when a Coach is charged with three technical fouls as a result of unsportsmanlike conduct by the Coach, Assistant Coach, or Team Follower, the Coach shall be disqualified and banished from the vicinity of the court. He shall be replaced by the Assistant Coach, or in the event of there not being an Assistant Coach, by the Captain.

B. Personal Contacts

Art. 79.   Personal Contact

Although Basketball is theoretically a **no-contact game,** it is obvious that personal contact cannot be avoided entirely when ten players are moving with great rapidity over a limited space. If personal contact results from a *bona fide* attempt to play the ball, provided the players are in such positions that they could reasonably expect to obtain possession of the ball without contact and if they use due care to avoid contact, such contact may be considered incidental and need not be penalised, unless it puts the player who has been contacted at a disadvantage (see art. 80).

On the other hand, if a player is about to catch the ball and an opponent behind him jumps in an attempt to get the ball and contacts him in the back, the opponent commits a foul, even though he is playing the ball. In such cases the player behind is usually responsible for the contact because of his unfavourable position in relation to the ball and his opponent.

183

Art. 80.   Personal Foul

A personal foul is a player foul which involves contact with an opponent whether the ball is in play, alive or dead.

A player shall not block, hold, push, charge, trip, impede the progress of an opponent by extending his arm, shoulder, hip or knee, or by bending his body into other than normal position, nor use any rough tactics.

Definitions:

Blocking: is personal contact which impedes the progress of an opponent who is not in control of the ball—*see Comments to art. 80.*

Holding is a personal contact with an opponent that interferes with his freedom of movement.

Pushing is personal contact that takes place when a player forcibly moves or attempts to move an opponent. Contact caused by a player approaching the ball holder from behind may be a form of pushing.

Guarding from the rear which results in personal contact is a personal foul. Officials should give special attention to this type of infraction. The mere fact that the defensive player is attempting to play the ball does not justify him in making contact with an opponent who controls the ball.

Charging is personal contact which occurs when a player, with or without the ball, makes his way forcibly and contacts an opponent in his path.

Illegal use of hands occurs when a player contacts an opponent with his hand(s) unless such contact is only with the opponent's hand while it is on the ball and is incidental to an attempt to play the ball.

Screening is an attempt to prevent an opponent who does not control the ball from reaching a desired position.

A dribbler shall not charge into nor contact an opponent in his path, nor attempt to dribble between opponents or between an opponent and a boundary line, unless there is a reasonable chance for him to go through without contact. If a dribbler without causing contact passes an opponent sufficiently to have head and shoulders in advance of him, the greater responsibility for subsequent contact is on the opponent. If a dribbler has established a straight line path, he may not be forced out of that path but if an opponent is able to establish a legal guarding position in that path, the dribbler must avoid contact by stopping or changing direction (*see Comments to art. 80*).

A player who screens has the greater responsibility if contact occurs when

(a) he takes a position so near an opponent that pushing or charging occurs when normal movements are made by him, or

(b) he takes a position so quickly in a moving opponent's path that pushing or charging cannot be avoided (*see Comments to art. 80*).

Penalty:

A personal foul shall be charged to the offender in all cases. In addition:

(1) *if the foul is committed on a player who is not in the act of shooting, the ball shall be put in play by the non-offending team from out-of-bounds on the side line nearest the place of the foul.*

As soon as the foul is called, the Official shall signal the Scorer the number of the offender and shall then hand the ball to the opponents for a throw-in from the side line (for exception, see art. 92, and also art. 90 and 93).

(2) *if the foul is committed on a player who is in the act of shooting:*

(i) *if the goal is made, it shall count, and, in addition, one free throw shall be awarded,*

(ii) *if the goal is missed, two free throws shall be awarded (see art. 89 and 90).*

(3) *As soon as the foul is called, the Official shall signal the Scorer the number of the offender and shall then place the ball at the disposal of the free thrower (see also art. 90).*

Art. 81.   Intentional Foul

An intentional foul is a personal foul which in the opinion of the Official was deliberately committed by a player.

A player who deliberately disregards the ball and causes personal contact with an opponent who controls the ball commits an **intentional foul.** This is generally true also of fouls committed on a player who does not have the ball. A player who **controls the ball** may also commit an intentional foul if he deliberately contacts an opponent. A player who repeatedly commits intentional fouls may be disqualified.

Penalty:

A personal foul shall be charged to the offender and, in addition, two free throws are awarded. However, if the foul is committed on a player who is in the act of shooting and scores, the basket shall count, and, in addition, one free throw shall be awarded (see art. 66, 80 and 89). If the foul is committed on a player in the act of shooting who fails to score, two free throws shall be awarded (see art. 66, 80, 89 and 90).

Art. 82.   Disqualifying Foul

Any flagrantly unsportsmanlike infraction of articles 77 and 80 is a disqualifying foul. A player who commits such a foul must be disqualified and removed immediately from the game and a foul shall be charged against him.

Penalty: *Same as art. 81.*

Art. 83.   Double Foul

A double foul is a situation in which two opponents commit fouls against each other at approximately the same time.

Penalty:

In case of a double foul, *no free throw shall be awarded but a personal foul shall be charged against each offending player.*

The ball shall be put in play *at the nearest circle by a jump-ball between the two players involved, unless a valid basket is scored at the same time, in which case the ball shall be put into play from the end line.* •

Art. 84.   Multiple Foul

A multiple foul is a situation in which two or more team mates commit personal fouls against the same opponent at approximately the same time.

Penalty:

When two or more personal fouls are committed against a player by opponents, one foul shall be charged to each offending player, and the offended player shall be awarded two free throws, irrespective of the number of fouls (see art. 89).

If the fouls are committed on a player in the act of shooting, the goal if made shall count and, in addition, one free throw shall be awarded.

Art. 85.   Foul on a Player in the Act of Shooting

Whenever a foul is called on the opponent of a player who, as part of a continuous motion which started before the foul occurred, succeeds in making a field goal, the goal shall count even if the ball leaves the player's hands after the whistle blows, provided the whistle did not affect the game. The player must be shooting for goal or starting an effort to shoot for goal when the whistle blows; the goal does not count if he makes an entirely new effort after the whistle blows.

C. General Provisions

Art. 86.   Basic Principle

Each Official has power to call fouls independently from the other, and this at any time during the game, whether the ball is in play, alive, or dead.

Fouls committed during the dead ball that follows a foul and until the moment when the ball is again in play (see art. 37) are considered as being committed at the time the ball became dead because of the first foul.

Any number of fouls may therefore be called at the same time against one or both teams. Irrespective of the penalty, a foul shall be inscribed on the Score Sheet against the offenders for each foul.

Art. 87.   Double and Multiple Foul

When a double foul and another foul are committed at the same time, the double foul shall be dealt with as in art. 83, and the other foul dealt with according to the respective Rule above. Play shall be resumed, after the fouls have been charged and the eventual penalty administered as though the double foul had not occurred.

Art. 88.   Fouls in Special Situations

Situations other than those foreseen in these Rules may occur when fouls are committed at approximately the same time or during the dead ball that follows a foul, a double foul, or a multiple foul.

As a general direction to Officials, the following principles may be applied in such situation:

(a) a foul shall be charged for each offence,

(b) fouls that involve penalties of about the same gravity against both teams shall not be penalised by awarding free throws, and the ball shall be put in play by a jump-ball at the nearest circle or, in case of doubt, at the centre,

(c) penalties that are not compensated by similar penalties against the other team shall be maintained but under no circumstances shall a team be awarded more than two free throws (see also art. 89) and possessions of the ball.

Art. 89.   Three-for-Two Rule

Whenever two free throws are awarded to a player who was fouled while in the act of shooting, if either or both these throws are unsuccessful, one additional free throw shall be awarded.

Art. 90.   Right of Option

A team that has been awarded two free throws (see also art. 89), shall have the option of either attempting the throws or of putting the ball in play from out-of-bounds at the **mid-point of a side line**.

The decision shall rest with the Captain of the team, who shall take the intiative to indicate immediately and clearly to the

Official in charge that the ball is to be put in play from the side line. A delay by Captain in using the right of option shall forfeit this right, and the two free throws shall be attempted.

The player who is to put the ball in play from out-of-bounds shall be entitled to pass the ball to a player at any point on the playing court.

The right of option shall not apply if a team has been awarded one or two free throws **and possession of the ball** (see art. 78 and 88-c).

Art. 91.   Five Fouls by Player
A player who has committed five fouls either personal or technical must automatically leave the game.

Art. 92.   Eight Fouls by Team
After a team has committed eight player fouls, personal or technical, in a half (extra periods are considered to be part of the second half) all subsequent player fouls shall be penalised by two free throws (for exceptions see art. 80, Penalty (2), art. 89 and also art. 93).

Art. 93.   Foul by Player whilst his Team is in Control of the Ball
A foul committed by a player whilst his team is in control of the ball shall always be penalised by recording the foul against the offender and awarding the ball to an opponent at the nearest point out-of-bounds at a side line (for exceptions, see art. 77 and 81).

Note — For definition of team in control of the ball see art. 49.

OFFICIAL BASKETBALL SIGNALS

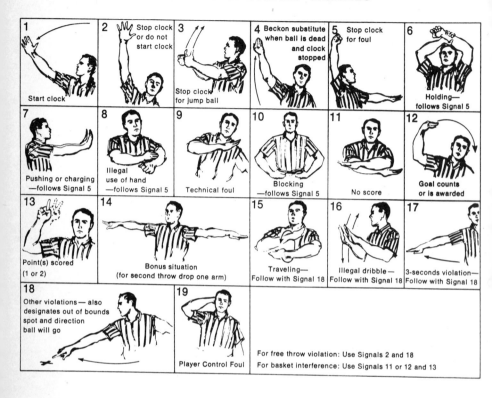

1. Start clock
2. Stop clock or do not start clock
3. Stop clock for jump ball
4. Beckon substitute when ball is dead and clock stopped
5. Stop clock for foul
6. Holding—follows Signal 5
7. Pushing or charging—follows Signal 5
8. Illegal use of hand—follows Signal 5
9. Technical foul
10. Blocking—follows Signal 5
11. No score
12. Goal counts or is awarded
13. Point(s) scored (1 or 2)
14. Bonus situation (for second throw drop one arm)
15. Traveling—Follow with Signal 18
16. Illegal dribble—Follow with Signal 18
17. 3-seconds violation—Follow with Signal 18
18. Other violations — also designates out of bounds spot and direction ball will go
19. Player Control Foul

For free throw violation: Use Signals 2 and 18
For basket interference: Use Signals 11 or 12 and 13

Index

Index